Beyond Eurocentrism and Multiculturalism: Volume I

Prophetic Thought in Postmodern Times

Cornel West

Common Courage Press • Monroe, Maine

Manufactured in the United States
ISBN 1-56751-004-3, paper   ISBN 1-56751-005-1, cloth

Common Courage Press
P.O. Box 702
Monroe, ME 04951
207-525-0900 fax: 207-525-3068

Library of Congress Cataloging in Publication Data
West, Cornel.
Beyond eurocentrism and multiculturalism / Cornel West.
    P. cm.
    Contents: v.1. Prophetic thought in postmodern times -- v. 2. Prophetic reflections
    ISBN 1-56751-005-1 (v. 1.) -- ISBN 1-56751-004-3 (pbk. : v. 1.) -- ISBN 1-56751-00708 (v. 2). -- ISBN 1-56751-006-X (pbk. : v. 2)
    1. United States--Race relations. 2. Pluralism (Social sciences)--United States. I. Title.
    E185.615.W425 1993
    305.8'00973--dc20   92-41610

Second Printing
The three speeches in Part I comprise the R. Grady Snuggs lectures given in October 1991 at the University of Tulsa.

"The Postmodern Crisis of Black Intellectuals" appeared in *Cultural Studies*, Grossberg, Nelson & Treichler, 1991.

"Decentring Europe: The Contemporary Crisis in Culture" appeared in *Critical Quarterly* Vol. 33 No. 1, Spring 1991.

The review of Jeffrey Stout's *Ethics After Babel* appeared in *Theology Today*, Vol. XLVI, No. 1, April 1989.

"Michael Harrington, Socialist," appeared in *The Nation*, January 8/15, 1990.

"Prospects for Democratic Politics: Reconstructing the Lippmann-Dewey Debate was given as a lecture in November 1990.

*To my best and beloved
friend
Professor James Melvin Washington
of Union Theological Seminary
New York City
who sticks close as a brother.*

Contents

Foreword *Irene and Clifton West*	vii
Introduction	ix

Part I
Prophetic Thought in Postmodern Times

Beyond Eurocentrism and Multiculturalism	3
Pragmatism and the Tragic	31
The Future of Pragmatic Thought	59

Part II
Contributions to Prophetic Pragmatism

The Postmodern Crisis of Black Intellectuals	87
Decentring Europe: The Contemporary Crisis in Culture	119
The Black Underclass and Black Philosophers	143
George M. Fredrickson & the Historiography of Race	159
On Walt Whitman	167
The Legacy of Raymond Williams	171
Jeffrey Stout's *Ethics After Babel*	175
Paulo Freire	179
Michael Harrington, Socialist	181
Prospects for Democratic Politics: Reconstructing the Lippmann-Dewey Debate	189

Foreword

There is one trophy among many that grace the bookshelves in our family room. This one was presented to an eleven year old seventh grader in 1964 for being the most inspirational member of the football team at Will C. Wood Jr. High School in Sacramento, California. Coach Jeffries had never given such a trophy before, but that year he felt it expedient because this bright, accelerated student had exuded such encouragement, was so positive, so upbeat that the morale of the team had been greatly enhanced as a result of his efforts and disposition. Little did we know that this gesture was the beginning of a lifetime of inspiration which would be sown into so many lives with whom this young man interacted.

High standards he set for himself academically, athletically, socially and spiritually. He always looked for the best of what others offered, shunning and downplaying the worst.

With members of his own family, his siblings, he focused on their best qualities and tried to strengthen the weaker traits. His sisters, Cynthia and Cheryl, two and six years his junior, respectively, always looked up to him with love and admiration. They begged their parents not to let him see their report cards for fear of disappointing him with any C's they may have received. Mind you, disappointment, not anger, for they knew his love and positivity was above that level.

His older brother, Clifton, three years his senior, always thought of him as a peer. His insatiable thirst to know as much as Clifton and to do what Clifton did was a given which Clifton accepted with admiration. Clifton was so secure in who he was that he was never intimidated by a younger brother who held him in such awe and wanted to be an integral part of his activities. Clifton's friends such as William Carr even accepted him as their equal. Throughout the years these brothers have grown even closer. They have looked over their younger sisters with loving and tender care.

At the tender age of sixteen he had been accepted at Harvard after having served as student body president of both his junior high school (following the steps of older brother) and senior high school (John F. Kennedy High School), first chair violinist in the school orchestra, very active and outspoken president of the Black Student Union, first-place winner in the two mile track event of the All-City Meet, played second base in the Baseball State Championship Game, officer in the California Scholarship Federation. In June 1970 he graduated with honors from high school six days after his 17th birthday. All of these were accomplished while simultaneously serving as an active member of Shiloh Baptist Church and Sacramento chapter of Jack & Jill of America, Inc.

As a member of the church and this civic and cultural organization, he voiced very strong convictions of what a Christian and community lay person ought to be about in eliminating or at least addressing, in some meaningful manner, the social ills of our society. He was very adamant then and has never waned throughout his adulthood in addressing these issues. We recollect when he and his brother, Clifton, were taken to the Memorial Auditorium to hear the late great Dr. Martin Luther King, Jr. He was about 9 or 10 years of age. He sat attentively listening to every word, absorbing each like a sponge. He cried when he told his sisters of what that experience had meant to him.

The person to whom we refer is the author. It is with utmost thankfulness in our hearts that we can unequivocally state that parenting this bright, high-spirited, loving and compassionate child was a challenge as well as a privilege. He has brought great joy and pride to our lives. We are richer for having had such an experience.

> Thy father and thy mother shall be glad, and she that bare thee shall rejoice.
>
> —Proverbs 23:25
>
> His parents
> Irene & Clifton West

Introduction

We live on the brink of a new wave of social activism in America. The defeat of the Bush administration unleashes new possibilities to enhance the plight of working and poor people in this country. Bill Clinton has shown that he is a clever and adroit politician. His pivotal victory should signify a crucial turn toward revitalizing the public spheres—from public health care, public education, public transportation to public conversation. Yet this turn will yield significant progress only if prophetic and progressive fellow citizens bring power and pressure to bear on the Clinton administration. Our regulative ideals are fourfold—a more egalitarian redistribution of wealth and power that includes the elimination of poverty, a head-on assault against white supremacist ideas and practices which embraces moral accountability of police power in the inner cities, a monumental pushing back of patriarchal and homophobic structures and a cultural renaissance that gives moral meaning and social hope for citizens in a more free, just—and ecologically sound—future.

As I travel across this nation I sense a deep hunger and thirst for a more compassionate country—one in which public service supercedes private opulence, institutional fairness triumphs over individual greed and the common good prevails over group xenophobia.

My aim in these two volumes is to present in clear, succinct and primarily *spoken* language a prophetic vision of what is worth fighting and dying for as this century comes to a close. I accent the *oral* character of these pieces not simply because most of them are uncut speeches and interviews, but also because they are efforts to connect in a more intimate way with fellow citizens in a conversational mode—much like a prophetic black preacher soliciting critical response from an open-minded yet suspicious congregation. The basic end is not to arrive at one correct solution to the myriad of problems, but rather to forge bonds of trust and to mutually empower one another to face the tragic facts of the past and present and respond to them in a flexible and courageous manner.

I have selected representative presentations out of the 150 lectures I give yearly at community centers, street corners, art museums, churches, synagogues, conferences, high schools, prisons, universities and on radio and TV. They range from talks in Tulsa, Chicago, Los Angeles, London, Paris, Soweto, Pittsburgh, Addis Ababa, Trenton, Burlington, Atlanta, Toronto, to Harlem.

The principle theme that echoes throughout the volumes is how and why we must go beyond eurocentrism and multiculturalism in order to keep alive prophetic thought and action in our time. For me, this means preserving the best of the black freedom struggle—a struggle that is a species of a radical democratic project that empowers and enhances the wretched of the earth. There are other forms of entree to this project in light of one's own history and heritage. Yet for all the freedom fighters, the unexamined life is not worth living and the examined life is a courageous struggle against all forms of ignorance and power that dehumanize people. This struggle is grounded in human love and human wisdom—the two fundamental requisites for the genuine flowering of we featherless, two-legged, linguistically conscious creatures made in the image of God.

I want to thank Janet Corpus and John Hoffmeyer for suggesting the idea of these volumes to the publisher. And I am grateful to the publisher—my friend Greg Bates—for suggesting the idea to me and executing the entire project.

Cornel West
December 1992

Part I
Prophetic Thought in Postmodern Times

Beyond Multiculturalism & Eurocentrism

I think it is very important as we reflect on prophetic thought in postmodern times, in these very, very deep and difficult crises of our day, to always view ourselves as part of a tradition. A long and grand tradition trying to forge a sense of dignity and decency, keeping alive quests for excellence and elegance. That is very much what I am. I stand very much on the shoulders of the deep love of my family. My mother and father and brothers and sisters.

My grandmother, who is here in Tulsa and who has been struggling and doing so very well and she is unable to be here today. We love her deeply because she gives us such inspiration. She is unable to be here because she is not well enough and yet she is still well enough to give us a sense of possibility. I talked to her until 3:00 a.m. last night. Already it was worth coming to Tulsa, just for that dialogue. Not that the dialogue with you won't be as rich, but if it is I will have a double blessing.

Let me begin, then by talking about prophetic thought in postmodern times and what it means to go beyond multiculturalism and eurocentrism. But I want to begin first by defining what I mean by the term "prophetic thought." There are four basic components, four fundamental features, four constitutive elements.

Discernment

The first element of prophetic thought has to do with discernment. Prophetic thought must have the capacity to provide a broad and deep analytical grasp of the present in light of the past. Discernment. We can call it an analytical moment. It is a moment in which one must accent a nuanced historical sense. What I mean by nuanced historical sense is an ability to keep track, to remain attuned to the ambiguous legacies and hybrid cultures in history.

This is very important as we shall see when we talk about multiculturalism and eurocentrism, because it means from the very beginning we must call into question any notions of pure traditions or pristine heritages, or any civilization or culture having a monopoly on virtue or insight. Ambiguous legacies, hybrid cultures. By hybrid, of course, we mean cross-cultural fertilization. Every culture that we know is a result of the weaving of antecedent cultures. Elements of antecedent cultures create something new based on that which came before.

This is so true of the United States, of course. There is no jazz without European instruments. But this is true all the way back to the beginning of the human adventure in Mesopotamia, Egypt and Pakistan, and Northern China off the Yellow River. So when we talk about Europe, we are not talking about anything monolithic or homogeneous. When we talk about multiculturalism we are talking about a particular critique of something which is already multicultural.

Which means that the very terms themselves, multi-culturalism and eurocentrism, are for me not analytical categories, they are categories to be analyzed with a nuanced historical sense, and also a subtle social analysis. By subtle social analysis, I mean powerful descriptions and persuasive explanations of wealth and status and prestige. We have to keep track at any social moment of who is bearing most of the social cost. This is what it means to look at the world from the vantage point of those below.

I believe, in fact, that the condition of truth is to allow the suffering to speak. It doesn't mean that those who suffer have a monopoly on truth, but it means that the condition of truth to emerge must be in tune with those who are undergoing social misery—socially induced forms of suffering.

Connection

This brings me to the second moment or constitutive element. It's about human connection. By this I mean a value of empathy. Empathy is something that is, unfortunately, waning in our time. Empathy is the capacity to get in contact with the anxieties and frustrations of others. To attempt to put yourself in their shoes. An attempt to get inside their skin.

There is a wonderful essay that William James wrote in 1903 upon the occasion of the U.S. invasion, occupation and annexation of the Philippines. It is called, "On a Certain Blindness in Human Beings." In this essay, William James raises the question of why it is that so many of his fellow citizens are unable to empathetically identify with Filipinos as human beings, but rather cast them as pictures and portraits—often stereotypical pictures and portraits.

The moment of human connection means never losing sight of the humanity of others. Always attempting to remain in contact with the humanity of others. It's a profoundly moral moment, this second component of the prophetic prospective.

Tracking Hypocrisy

The third moment is one of what we could call loosely, keeping track of human hypocrisy, in a self-critical, not a self-righteous mode. By keeping track of human hypocrisy, I mean accenting boldly, and defiantly, the gap between principles and practice, between promise and performance, between rhetoric and reality.

It has to do with courage because one must take a risk in pointing out human hypocrisy, and one must point out human hypocrisy while remaining open to having others point out that of your own. This is why it is self-critical. This is why a conception of the prophetic in our time cannot be one that claims we have unmediated access to God. But, rather, we are fallen vessels through which more critique is brought to bear on ourselves. We are often complicit with the very thing we are criticizing. It is a form of intellectual humility. But it still takes a stand.

Hope

The last moment, the fourth moment, is one of human hope. And hope, for me, is one of the most difficult things to talk about in the latter part of the twentieth century. What a ghastly century we have lived in. So many millions of people whose lives have been taken or their life's chances crushed.

And there are so many hope peddlers who are manipulative, charlatan-like, blinding, obscuring. And yet, we must talk about hope. To talk about human hope is to engage in an audacious attempt to galvanize and energize, to inspire and to invigorate world-weary people. Because that is what we are. We are world-weary; we are tired. For some of us there are misanthropic skeletons hanging in our closet. And by misanthropic I mean the notion that we have given up on the capacity of human beings to do *anything* right. The capacity of human communities to solve any problem.

We must face that skeleton as a challenge, not a conclusion. But be honest about it. Weary, and keep alive the notion that history is incomplete, that the world is unfinished, that the future is open-ended and that what we think and what we do can make a difference.

If you give up on that notion then there is no hope and all you have is sophisticated analysis. Ironic reflection. Even narcissistic forms of intellectual engagement. If you don't think what you think and what you do can make a difference, then the possibility of human hope wanes.

Multiculturalism and Eurocentrism

Given these four components, then, how are we to think about multiculturalism and eurocentrism? I am sure that most of you know that there has been a lot of talk about multiculturalism these days. It is a buzzword. It is often undefined. It tends to function in a rather promiscuous manner, to lie down with any perspective, any orientation. So we need to handle it. It is a rather elusive and amorphous term.

The same is true with eurocentrism. What do we mean by eurocentrism? Which particular European nation do you have in mind? Which classes of europeans do you have in mind? Certainly, Sicilian peasants don't have the same status as Oxbridge elites. What Europe do you have in mind?

We begin with the first moment of this lecture. There are three historical coordinates that will help us "situate and contextualize" this debate that is going on, as Brother John [Bolin who introduced this lecture series] puts it.

The Value of the Age of Europe

The first historical coordinate is the fact that we have yet to fully come to terms with the recognition that we live 48 years after the end of the Age of Europe. Between 1492 and 1945, powerful nations between the Ural mountains and the Atlantic Ocean began to shape the world in their own image. Break throughs in oceanic transportation, break throughs in agricultural production, break throughs in the consolidation of nation status, break-throughs in urbanization, led toward a take-off.

1492, the problem of degrading other people and the expulsion of Jews and Muslims and wars in Spain. 1492, Christopher Columbus shows up in what to him is a New World. It is not new to indigenous peoples; they have been there for thousands of years, two hundred nations, as those of you who are here tonight in Tulsa know quite intimately.

But the New World concept was part of an expansionism, keeping in mind our ambiguous legacies. We don't want to romanticize and we don't want to trivialize. There were structures of domination already here before the Europeans got here. The plight of indigenous women, for example. It doesn't mean that the wiping out of indigenous peoples by disease and conquest somehow gets European conquistadors off the hook. But it means that there was always, already, oppression. In new forms it was brought.

1492, publication of the first grammar book in Indo-European languages by Antonio de Nebrija in Spanish. Language, of course, being the benchmark in the foundation of a culture. This is what is so interesting about multiculturalism these days. The fact that the dialogue takes place in English already says something. For me, English is an imperial language. My wife is Ethiopian and she dreams in Amharic. I dream in English. That says something about us culturally. We still love each other, but it says something about us culturally. Namely, that I am part of a profoundly hybrid culture. I happen to speak the very language of the elite who tell me that I am not part of the human family, as David Walker said in his Appeal of September 1829. And she speaks Amharic, a different elite, in a different empire, an Ethiopian empire. Different hybridity. Different notions about what it means to be multicultural in this regard.

1492, a crucial year. Between 1492 and 1945, we see unprecedented levels of productivity. We see what, in my view, is the grand achievement of the Age of Europe. Because it was in some way marvelous, and it was in some other ways quite ugly. What was marvelous about it was the attempt to institutionalize critiques of illegitimate forms of authority. Let me say that slowly: The attempt to hammer out not just critical gestures but critiques that could be sustained of arbitrary forms of power. That's what the Reformation was about in its critique of the Catholic Church.

Think what you will about Martin Luther. He was bringing critique to bear on what he perceived to be arbitrary forms of power. That is what the Enlightenment was about, fighting against national churches that had too much unaccountable power leading to too many lives crushed. That's what liberalism was about against absolute monarchy. That is what women's movements are about against male authority. That's what anti-racist movements are about against white supremacist authority.

They are building on traditions of critique and resistance. And, during the age of Europe, given levels of productivity, there were grand experiments. Each and every one of them flawed, but grand experiments to try to live in large communities while institutionalizing critiques of illegitimate forms of authority. This was the makings of the democratic ideal, to which accountability to ordinary people became not just an abstract possibility, but realizable. As I say, it was deeply flawed.

The greatest experiment as we know, began in 1776. But they were institutionalizing these critiques. It didn't apply to white men who had no property. It didn't apply to women. It didn't apply to slaves, people of African descent in the United States who were 21 percent of the population at that time. But that is not solely the point. It is in part the point. But it is not fully the point. The courageous attempt to build a democratic experiment in which the uniqueness of each and every one of us, the sanctity of each and every one of us who has been made equal in the eyes of God becomes at least possible.

That democratic idea is one of the grand contributions of the Age of Europe even given the imperial expansion, the colonial subjugation of Africa and Asia, the pernicious and vicious crimes against working people and people of color and so forth. So ambiguous legacy means, in talking about multiculturalism, we have got to keep two ideas in our minds at the same time. The achievements as well as the downfalls. The grand contributions and the vicious crimes.

The End of the Age of Europe
And the Rise of the United States

1945. The Age of Europe is over. Europe is a devastated and divided continent. Mushroom clouds over Nagasaki and Hiroshima. Indescribable concentration camps in Germany. Again, Europe's inability to come to terms with the degradation of others. Now upon the hills of a divided continent emerges the first new nation. The U.S.A. Henry James called it a "hotel civilization." A hotel is a fusion between the market and the home. The home, a symbol of warmth and security, hearth. The market, dynamic, mobile, the quest for comfort and convenience. Both home and market. Deeply privatistic phenomenon. By privatistic, I mean being distant from, even distrustful of, the public interest and the common good.

In the first new nation, American civilization with tremendous difficulty was trying to define its national identity. What ought to be the common interest. What ought to be the common good. It is quite striking in fact that this first new nation doesn't even raise the question of what it means to be a citizen until after the Civil War, when they have to decide what is the status of the freed men and women, the ex-enslaved persons. The first new nation, a heterogenous population. People come from all around the world. In quest for what? Opportunity. In quest for what? A decent life. The quest for what? More comfort and convenience.

In 1945, we thought it would be—not "we," but Henry Luce did at least—the American Century. It only lasted 28 years. For the first time in human history, Americans created a modern social structure that looks like a diamond rather than a pyramid. Mass middle class, owing to the GI Bill, Federal Housing Administration programs, Workers' Compensation, Unemployment Compensation. The Great Society that played such a fundamental role in moving persons from working class to middle class in the United States. And yet, the distinctive feature of American civilization in its negative mode, would be the institutionalizing of a discourse of whiteness and blackness.

The issue of race. Race is not a moral mistake of individuals, solely. It is a feature of institutions and structures that insures that one group of people have less access to resources, both material and intangible. By material, I mean money, housing, food, health care. By intangible, I mean things like self-confidence. I mean things like self-respect and self-regard and self-esteem. The discourse of whiteness and blackness would result in the incessant bombardment of people of color. Attacks on black beauty. Attacks on black intelligence. You can still get tenure in some universities for arguing that black people are not as intelligent as others. Where did that come from?

We are not concerned about eye color, not concerned about the shape of ears. But we are still concerned about pigmentation. It has a history. Of attacks on black intelligence. Attacks on black possibility. What is fascinating about this discourse, that in many ways is distinctive to the USA, though South Africa shares it as well, is that those who came to the United States didn't realize they were white until they got here. They were told they were white. They had to learn they were white. An Irish peasant coming from British imperial abuse in Ireland during the potato famine in the 1840s, arrives in the States. You ask him or her what they are. They say "I am Irish." No, you're white. "What do you mean I am white?" And they point me out. Oh, I see what you mean. This is a strange land.

Jews from Ukraine and Poland and Russia undergoing ugly pogroms, assaults and attacks, arrive in Ellis Island. They are told they have to choose, either white or black. They say neither, but they are perceived as white. They say I will not go with the goyim, the goyim have treated me like whites treat black people here. But, I am certainly not black either.

This is the 1880s. This is a time in which that peculiar American institution in which a black woman, a man, a child was swinging from a tree every two and a half days for thirty years. An institution unique to the United States called lynching, that "strange fruit that Southern trees bear" which Billy Holiday sang so powerfully about. It's happening every other day. And many Jews would say, no baby, I'm sure not identifying with these folk.

Arbitrary use of power. Unaccountable. Segregated laws, Jim and Jane Crow unaccountable. But yet, this new nation, after 1945, would emerge to the center of the historical stage. We now come to the third historical coordinate, the first was the end of the Age of Europe, the second was the emergence of the United States as a world power, and the third is the decolonization of the Third World.

The Decolonization of the Third World

By decolonization, I mean the quest of colonized people around the world, between 1945 and 1974, to break the back of European maritime empires. 1947, India. Exemplary anti-colonial struggle. Young preacher, 26 years old, Dexter Avenue Baptist Church, Montgomery, Alabama. He and couragous others look to India for anti-colonial strategy. Nonviolent struggle. Applies the same techniques and strategies to try to break the back of an apartheid-like rule of law in the United States.

The civil rights movement was part of a larger international attempt to bring critiques to bear on the empire building that had taken place during the heyday of the Age of Europe namely the nineteenth century. '47 India, '49 China, '57 Ghana, '59 Cuba, '60 Guinea. We go on and on and on. '74 Angola. South Africa as yet to come. There is no way, of course, of looking past some of the colossal failures of the post-colonial regimes in some of those places, or the greed and corruption of the post-colonial elites, like Moi in Kenya, or Mengistu in Ethiopia, or Mobutu. The list is long.

But the decolonization points out the degree to which we are living in a fundamentally different world. In 1945, the UN had 45 nations; there are now 172 and there will be more soon given the disintegration of the Soviet Empire. It is a different world.

This is a way of situating broadly what the debate between multiculturalism and eurocentrism is about. But it forces us to call into question anyone who would criticize eurocentrism, as if, as I said before, it is monolithic. Because there are struggles going on in Europe between a whole host of different peoples with different cultures and different nations. And one has to begin with a nuanced historical sense in laying bare a genealogy or a history of the very term Europe itself.

Before the debate begins, when was Europe used for the first time as a noun? Christmas, 800, Charles the Great. Pope Leo III puts the crown upon his head. There's only Lombards and the Franks. Two out of eight clans. No Alamans. No Bavarians. An attempt to impose a unity from above. Arab caliphs threatening, Empress Irene in Greek Christendom. Unstable. Historians tell us that without Mohammed, Charlemagne would have been inconceivable. That is what Henri Pirenne says in his magisterial reading of this moment. And yet, at the same time, the attempt to conceive of Europe as some kind of homogenous entity collapses. 843. Partition. At Verdun. Territorial principalities. Their particularisms. Their multiplicities expand and surface. Europe as an entity is not taken seriously.

Second attempt, 1458. Pope Pius II, five years after the Turkish invasion of Constantinople. Responding to the Turkish menace, Europe is attempting to forge some collective identity. Reformation. Churches under national government, particularism again. Multiplicity again.

Last attempt made, 1804. Napoleon puts crown on his own head. And he calls himself not Emperor of Europe, but Emperor of France.

Francis II, withdrew himself as Emperor, and said I am simply part of Austria now. After May, 1804, the collapse of Napoleon and we see the emergence of nationalism. A new tribalism in the human adventure. A nationalism that would strain the moral imagination. Populations around the world remain to this day in this central tribal division of humankind.

That is what is going on in Yugoslavia, that is what is going on in Russia. That is what is going on in Ethiopia between the Tigrans and the Amhara, and the Oromo. Nationalism. And, this nationalism would dictate the rules of power during the heyday of the Age of Europe. So strong that people would be willing die for it. That is pretty deep. That is pretty deep, that we all have to impose or endow some sense of meaning to our lives and one test is what we are willing to die for. And citizens around the world are willing to die for their nation-state. That's how deep the thread of nationalism is. That particular form of tribalism. And by calling it tribalism, I am not using that in a degrading sense. Because all of us are born under circumstances not of our own choosing, in particular families, clans, tribes and what-have-you. We all need protection. Tribes protect. Nation-states protect.

We all need identity. Tribes provide identity. But, of course, prophetic critique, and of course, in my view the Christian version of the prophetic critique, is that when any form of tribalism becomes a form of idolatry, then a critique and resistance must be brought to bear. When any form of tribalism becomes a justification for hiding and concealing social misery, critique and resistance must be brought to bear.

Economic & Social Decline

Let's come closer in our first moment of discernment. In our present moment here, and I will be saying more about this in the last lecture, but I want to touch on this now. From 1973 to 1989 was a period of national decline. For the first time since the '30s. Levels of productivity nearly freeze. A 0.4 percent increase in 1973-4.

There are reasons that we need not go into as to fragility of the debt structure linked to Third World nations. It has much to do, of course, with the rise of OPEC and the Third World monopoly of one of the crucial resources of the modern world, oil. We saw that in January [1991, during the Gulf War]. I think most of us are convinced that if the major resource of Kuwait was artichokes we would not have responded so quickly.

Which doesn't take away from the rhetoric of the liberation of Kuwait. Kuwaitis were, in fact, living under vicious and repressive regime under Sadaam Hussein. But there are a whole lot of regimes where people are living that we don't respond to. The rise of OPEC in '74 made a fundamental difference. The slowdown of the U.S. economy. No longer expanding. The unprecedented economic boom no longer in place. And since 1974, the real wages—by real wages I mean inflation-adjusted wages of non-supervisory workers in America—have declined. Which means social slippage, which means downward mobility that produces fear.

Material uncertainty becomes real. As you can imagine, it serves as a raw ingredient for scapegoating. And from '73 to '89, we have seen much scapegoating. The major scapegoats have been women and black people, especially at the behest of certain wings of the Republican Party. We don't want to tar the Republican Party as a whole, but yes indeed, in '68 Nixon was talking about busing as a racially coded term. Harry Dent, the same architect of the strategy that led to the walkout of Strom Thurmond in 1948, due to the civil rights plank in the party, and the formation of the Dixiecrats. The same Harry Dent who served as the principal architect in '48 and lingered in '68.

Kevin Phillips wrote a book in '69 called *The New Republican Majority* which is an appeal to race to convince white working class ethnic workers that black people were receiving too much and were unjustified in what they were receiving and that whites were getting a raw deal and ought to come to the Republican Party.

Thomas and Mary Edsall tell the story in their recent *Chain Reaction. The impact of rights and race and taxes on American politics*. '76 the Democrats ride on the coattails of Watergate, but they have very little substance. In '80, Ronald Reagan consolidates it all and begins his campaign in Philadelphia, Mississippi and says state rights forever. Racially coded language. Political realignment. The Republican Party becomes essentially a lily-white party. Which is not to say that all Republicans are racist. It is a lily-white party.

Another feature is inadequate education for workers so that the products that they produce cannot compete. Japan, Taiwan and South Korea surge. Even Brazil. Stubborn incapacity to generate resources for the public square. No New Taxes, read my lips. Inability to generate resources means public squalor alongside private opulence.

The Ravages of the Culture of Consumption

Added to these problems is the undeniable cultural decay, which is in fact quite unprecedented in American history. This is what frightens me more than anything else. By unprecedented cultural decay I mean the social breakdown of the nurturing system for children. The inability to transmit meaning, value, purpose, dignity, decency to children.

I am not just talking about the one out of five children who live in poverty. I am not just talking about the one out of two black and two out of five brown children who live in poverty. I am talking about the state of their souls. The deracinated state of their souls. By deracinated I mean rootless. The denuded state of their souls. By denuded, I mean culturally naked. Not to have what is requisite in order to make it through life. Missing what's needed to navigate through the terrors and traumas of death and disease and despair and dread and disappointment. And thereby falling prey to a culture of consumption. A culture that promotes addiction to stimulation. A culture obsessed with bodily stimulation. A culture obsessed with consuming as the only way of preserving some vitality of a self.

You are feeling down, go to the mall. Feeling down, turn on the TV. The TV with its spectator passivity. You are receiving as a spectator, with no sense of agency, no sense of making a difference. You are observing the collapse of an empire and feeling unable to do anything about it, restricted to just listening to Dan Rather talk about it. A market culture that promotes a market morality.

A market morality has much to do with the unprecedented violence of our social fabric. The sense of being haunted every minute of our lives in our homes and on the street. Because a market morality puts money-making, buying and selling, or hedonistic self-indulgence at the center of one's behavior. Human life has little value. I want it, I want it now. Quick fix, I've got the gun, give it to me. It affects us all. I know some people try to run and move out to the suburbs and the technoburbs and so forth, but it effects us all. Market morality.

We should keep in mind that one of the great theorists of market society, namely Adam Smith, wrote a book in 1776, *The Wealth of Nations.* It is a powerful book in many ways. He talked about ways in which you generate wealth, but he also wrote a book in 1759 called *The Theory of Moral Sentiments.* And in that book Adam Smith argues that a market culture cannot sustain a market economy.

You need market forces as necessary conditions for the preservation of liberties in the economy. But when the market begins to hold sway in every sphere of a person's life, market conceptions of the self, market conceptions of time, you put a premium on distraction over attention, stimulation over concentration, then disintegrate sets in. Also in this book, Adam Smith talks about the values of virtue and propriety, and especially the value of sympathy that he shared with his fellow Scot, David Hume. And when these nonmarket values lose influence or when their influence wanes, then you have got a situation of Hobbes' war of all against all, of cultural anarchy and social chaos.

Emile Durkheim put it another way, put it well when he said that a market culture evolves around a notion of contract, but every contractual relation presupposes pre-contractual commitments. So, a contract means nothing if there is no notion of truth telling and promise keeping. It has no status. It collapses. Now all we have is manipulative relations. I don't know how many of you have been reading Michael Levine's book, *The Money Culture*. I don't want to make an advertisement for it, but the book looks at what happens when a market culture begins to take over the center of a person's life. It tells stories about a Wall Street speculator who is upset because he only made 550 million dollars in a year. He has got to make 555, and he is willing to take a risk and break the law to do it.

You say, what is going on? It cannot be solely a question of pointing fingers at individuals. We are talking about larger cultural tendencies that affect each and every one of us. It takes the form of self-destructive nihilism in poor communities, in very poor communities. The lived experience of meaninglessness and hopelessness and lovelessness. Of self-paralyzing pessimism among stable working-class and lower working-class people in which they feel as if their life, their standard of living is declining, they are convinced that the quality of life is declining. And yet, they are looking for quick solutions. I think in part that is what David Duke is all about. It is not just that the people who support him are racist, though, of course, many are. It's that they are looking for a quick solution to a downward slide they experience in their lives. He speaks to it in his own xenophobically coded language. The racist coded language. He is gaining ground.

There is a self-indulgent hedonism and self-serving cynicism for those at the top. To simply let it collapse and pull back. Public school, nothing to do with it. Public transportation, nothing to do with it. Public health, nothing to do with it. Privatize them because I have access to resources that allow me to privatize in such a way that I can have quality. The rest, do what you will, make it on your own.

In such a context, is it a surprise then, that we see tribal frenzy and xenophobic strife? Multiculturalism and eurocentrism; two notions that go hand in hand. Our attempts on the one hand to respond to the tribal frenzy and xenophobic strife, and yet in their vulgar versions they contribute to it. These are highly unfortunate times which prepackage a debate resulting in even more polarization because it obscures and obfuscates what is fundamentally at stake in our moment. Intellectually, as I noted before, this means preserving the nuanced historical sense. But how do you preserve a historical sense in a market culture that effaces the past? A past that comes back to us through televisual means solely in the form of icons.

You go into any school today, who are the great figures? Martin Luther King, Jr. That is fine. Can you tell me something about the context that produced him. There is no King without a movement, there is movement without King. King is part of a tradition. But all we have is icons. George Washington. Icon. He was part of an armed revolutionary movement. He picked up guns and threw out the British imperialists. And he tried to institutionalize his conception of democracy. Grand but flawed, as I said before.

How do we preserve a sense of history in such a moment? What a challenge. But this is what is intellectually at stake. It makes no sense. Students read Toni Morrison and simply look in her text and see themselves rather than the challenge of a great artist who is dealing with collective memory and community breakdown in *Beloved*, for example. Challenge. If you look in a text and see yourself, that is market education, done in the name of education. But education must not be about a cathartic quest for identity. It must foster credible sensibilities for an active critical citizenry.

How do we preserve critical sensibility in a market

culture? In our churches, in our synagogues, in our mosques, they are often simply marketing identity. It must be a rather thin identity, this market. It won't last long. Fashion, fad. Someone benefitting, usually the elites who do the marketing and benefitting. How deep does one's identity cut? Most importantly, what is the moral content of one's identity? What are the political consequences of one's identity? These are the kinds of questions that one must ask in talking about multiculturalism and eurocentrism.

If one is talking about critiques of racism, critiques of patriarchy, critiques of homophobia, then simply call it that. Eurocentrism is not identical with racism. So, you deny the John Brown's of the world. You deny the anti-racist movement in the heart of Europe. Eurocentrism is not the same as male supremacists. Why? Because every culture we know has been patriarchal in such an ugly way and that you deny the anti-patriarchal movements within the heart of Europe. And the same is so with homophobia. Demystify the categories in order to stay tuned to the complexity of the realities. That is what I am calling for. That is the role of prophetic thinkers and prophetic activists who are willing to build on discernment, human connection. Who are willing to hold up human hypocrisy, including their own and also willing to hold up the possibility of human hope.

What I shall attempt to do tomorrow [in the second lecture] is to look at a distinctive American tradition that makes democracy its object of focus, its object of investigation, namely, American pragmatism. And pragmatism has nothing to do with practicalism or opportunism, which is the usual meaning of that term which you see in your newspapers. So and so was pragmatic. No principles, just did what had to be done. No, no. That is not what we will be talking about. American pragmatism is a distinct philosophical tradition that begins with Charles Sanders Peirce, through William James, through John Dewey, and Sidney Hook and W. E. B. Du Bois, all the way up to the present. And, it makes democracy a basic focus.

Its fundamental focus and question is, what are the prospects of democracy? How do you promote individuality and allow it to flower and flourish? I will be linking this tradition with the deep sense of the tragic, which I think the pragmatic tradition lacks. I will try to show ways in which Christian resources can be brought to bear to keep track of the sense of the tragic without curtailing agency. Without curtailing possibilities for action and then I will end [in the third lecture] with what the future of prophetic thought looks like. And I will try to answer some of those questions about whether indeed we can even talk about preserving a historical sense and subtle analysis in a culture that is so saturated by market sensibilities. Thank you so very much.

Questions & Comments

Question: Would you elaborate as to why 1973 is one of the significant dates?

West: That is the year of the end of the unprecedented economic boom in the United States beginning in 1945. That is when the slowdown begins. As I said before, that is the year that had only a 0.4 percent increase in productivity. And what is fascinating is to acknowledge the prior economic boom, the 1960s, which had so much social strife and so on. You have to deal with 329 revolts in 257 cities between 1964 and 1968 during this period. But it was a period, also, of tremendous economic expansion. Low inflation, low unemployment.

In 1973 we had increased inflation, increased unemployment. Phillips' Curve doesn't work anymore. Something else is going on. Part of it had to do with the challenge of the Japanese and the West Germans who would later unify, as we know. It had to with the challenge of Brazil in certain spheres, like shoe production and so on, and it also had to do with, as I said before, the bank structure.

As the loans to Third World nations began to escalate, the banks felt more and more ill at ease and what we had then was an economic restructuring in the United States between 1973 and about 1984. That restructuring was primarily twofold. It was deregulation and deindustrialization. Deindustrialization meant that we dismantled our industrial production units and put them in other parts of the world where labor was cheaper. So production collapsed. Auto production slowed. Rubber production collapsed. These are some of the basic pillars of American industry. I'm not talking about post-industrial production, like Silicon Valley, computerization, robotization, and so on, but old style industrial manufacturing units in Youngstown and Akron, Ohio.

And then the deregulation, of course, meant that you allowed relatively unbuffeted markets to take over and hence speculation, mergers, takeovers increased. The smaller fish were devoured by the larger ones, as in the airline industry and so on. And it also meant decrease in safety as we also know.

There was relative recovery. There is no doubt about that. But the recovery itself was skewed. Recovery had more to do with upper-middle-class jobs in which their salaries and incomes increased exponentially. At the same time there was regressive taxation. Moving from a 70 percent bracket for top earners down to 28 percent.

And there was an increase in part-time jobs, usually with no pensions and no benefits. Burger King, McDonald's kinds of jobs that were primarily for older people and for young people who had in common that they were vulnerable in the job market, and who tend to be disproportionately people of color. They are mainly revolving jobs. No serious solidity and longevity. So, it was a partial recovery under Reagan and early Bush. And so it is a period in which any time any nation gets social breakdown in the nurturing of children, and downward mobility along with spiritual impoverishment. That is a lethal combination. And that is what I am fighting against. That is a sign of decline of any empire that we know.

As I shall talk about tomorrow, America has always been a nation that looked to the future. It is a prospective nation. That is one of the reasons why we have such a limited sense of history, that we are a forward-looking nation rather than a backward-looking nation.

Spain is backward looking. Italy is backward looking. Do you remember that battle in 1341 and so on. 1341 in America means a lotto number. That is a different orientation. We are forward looking. But when those systems begin to break down and no longer nurture the very inhabitants of our future, it means they can no longer look at the future in a positive manner. Then you have got something new on your hands. Very new on your hands. And you begin to see anomie becoming more pervasive. Homicide, suicide especially. But homicide as well. And a whole host of other indices of social anomie.

It is not, as I noted before, a question solely of individual motivation. It is, in part, individual motivation, because individuals have responsibility for their actions. But we are talking about larger cultural trends and tendencies. And we first have to analyze and discern what is going on as we then bring vision to bear, attempt to bring people of good will together to do something about it, because we are all in the same boat, as it were, whether we like it or not.

King used to say we are all part of one garment of destiny, one inextricable network of mutuality and we have to acknowledge that. We are whether we like each other or not.

Question: What institutions do you see as most hopeful to address this problem?

West: I think we have to look at both the past and the future for this. What I mean is this: When we look at the past, certainly it is going to be religious institutions that can play a crucial role. For me, the church is a very important institution in this regard. But the prophetic church. Because, of course, we have market religion, too. Prayers that become Let's Make a Deal with God, the sermon becomes the next commercial for J.C. and so on.

So we have to bring critique to bear on market influences in the church so that the content of the gospel doesn't get flattened out. So that the message of the Cross doesn't become diluted. So that the preacher doesn't become just another businessman. That is a serious struggle. But I do believe that prophetic churches, prophetic mosques, prophetic synagogues can all play a fundamental role in nurturing children by transmitting non-market values. I will be talking about that love, care, service to others, sacrifice, risk, community, struggles for justice, solidarity, all of these are non-market values against a market culture.

But when I say look to the future, there is not going to be solely institutions of civil society like churches, but the other institutions that may emerge as well. And we just don't know. One way of talking about this theologically is that we believe that there always will be a cloud of witnesses, but we don't know what form it will take. If the churches and religious institutions fail, then the spirit will go somewhere else because the rocks will cry out if they don't. I believe that. I could be naive, of course, but I believe that. So that there may be new forms.

Similarly, there may be new forms in terms of families. Oftentimes, when people talk about non-market values, we talk about family, we presuppose patriarchal families. There is no return to patriarchal families in my view, both on historical grounds and on moral and religious grounds. Women aren't going to put up with it. That is good. They shouldn't have never put up with it. But that doesn't mean that we must not come up with other relations of love, care and nurturing. You can't simply have an abstract critique of the patriarchal family without replacing what was in place with something that also nourishes.

People don't live on arguments. They might be influenced by arguments, we hope. But, they don't live on arguments. They live on love, care, respect, touch, and so forth. So, then it becomes incumbent upon those of us, the feminist movement and those who support them with goodwill, to come up with relations of nurturing that are de-patriarchalized. Which is to say, more equal between sexes, but also solid enough to produce the next generation. And that is where debate takes place.

What forms of childcare are we talking about? Is it only childcare in the public sphere? Are there ways, in fact, for providing flexible hours such that childcare could be one in which parents have a closer link to the child, even as that parent still works? And so forth and so on. Those are the kinds of questions we have to raise in looking at those institutions of the past and those new institutions that will emerge. I would like to see the egalitarian family emerge as a paradigm, for example. That is hope, but one pushes for that kind of thing.

I think the same is going to be true in terms of mass culture. As you know, young people these days are much more socialized and acculturated by mass culture than they are by family. It's by TV, video. And TV and video put a premium on the deployment of women's bodies to stimulate, for the most part. And not just any women's bodies. My view is that they don't have enough dark skinned women's bodies even in those vulgar videos. That says something about ideals of beauty that are problematic for me. You see what I mean. Not that I just want the dark sisters to be in there to be exploited, but this says something about ideals of beauty that the black videos always have a certain kind of women in them. What is going on? But within mass culture, there will be more forms, new forms that we may not even conceive of.

I think of Spike Lee's films, for example. And the degree to which his films now become sources of public conversation the way James Baldwin's essays used to be. Now, unfortunately, not as good as James Baldwin's essays, but that is another question. But, they become serious sites for conversation. Barber shops, beauty parlors, on the street and so forth. What do you think of Spike's *Mo' Better Blues*?

What do you think of Spike's *Jungle Fever*? Get dialogues going. We need that. We need to have dialogue. Film will become a very important tool in this regard. Which is very different from what we have seen in the past in the black community for example.

Television, I think, will also play this role. Arsenio Hall, for example, as silly as he can be and insightful as he can be all at the same time, has become a very important new space. Even though much of the show is about advertisement. Almost everybody he brings in has got a new show out, here is the clip. Got a new show out, here is the clip. That is as market as it can be. They have a conversation, here is the clip. But, there are some possibilities there too for serious reflection on issues. Spiritual sterility, and spiritual nourishment. Political engagement, prophetic critique and so on. So that the long, long answer to your question is we have to look both to the past and the present.

Question: [Inaudible.]

West: I appreciate that question, it is a very good one. Should I restate the question? It had to do with the rise of interest in Afrocentricity. One example would be Molefi Asante. The interest in Africa is a response to the degradation of African peoples, especially during the Age of Europe. And the question was, how would one build on some of the insights of this new interest and what particular forms would it take? Is that a fair restatement of what you were asking? How would one ensure that the movement would last longer than Garvey's movement, or Negritude, or the Harlem Renaissance, or the '60s black art movement and how did it impact on non-African peoples? That is a good question.

I think there are two very, very positive elements of Afrocentricity that I want to stress before I come to the critique of it. The first is to acknowledge the degradation of things African during the Age of Europe. And this is very, very important. It is undeniable, of course, but it's important that one never loses sight of that and it has to be acknowledged. The second is something I think speaks to the breakdown in those institutions in the black community, the institutions that promoted forms of self-regard and self-respect and self-love. That is, the erosion of those institutions has led to a hunger and thirst for black self-love. And that is very real. You see it in hip hop culture, and rap music. You see it in intellectual movements like Afrocentricity and so on.

The question becomes, then, how does one build upon those elements while trying to avoid certain traps? On the one hand, of course, the first move is, if you are concerned about the degradation of things African by Europeans, then you don't simply want to degrade non-African things in order to make Africans look good. That would be imitating the worst of European civilization. If you are concerned about promoting mature forms of self-love and self-regard, it means that we have to come up with way of promoting self-love and self-regard without putting down others. And I think we have paradigms for that. Jazz is one paradigm. That is a very good one. You see Charlie Parker didn't have to worry about whether he thought his music was linked to Africa, linked to monuments or linked to Europe. He just played his music and people listened. Because it was building on a tradition that didn't put whiteness on a pedestal, nor did it put whiteness in the gutter. He actually believed that white people were simply human beings like anybody else. You see, for oppressed people that is hard to admit. Because the propensity is to demonize or deify. If you have a narrow assimilationist position, then you deify. Put whiteness on a pedestal. Whiteness is good. The closer I get the better I feel. There is a tradition in black America like that.

And the flip side is to put whiteness in the gutter, you see. It ain't no good, it ain't never made no contribution for nobody, treated me like a dog, and so forth and so on. That treatment like a dog is real. But whether in fact, one's humanity is completely fleshed out only to the degree that one engages in devilish behavior is a different question.

28   PROPHETIC THOUGHT IN POSTMODERN TIMES

You can talk about devilish behavior without inferring that people are devils. They are just human beings that act devilishly. And there are a lot of white folk around who fit that in the last 150 years. No doubt about that. There are some black ones, too. A lot of white folk around who fit that now. We can testify to that. There is no doubt about that.

I was telling Brother John today the real sense in which this university (TU) changed my life, and changed my father's life. His name was submitted to this institution so he could stay in town in order to raise his family. He applied and couldn't get in even though he had straight A's on his report card because TU wasn't accepting black folk, and he took off for Kansas and ended up in California. Now, in one instance, I am glad because I like sunny California. But in another sense, we are talking about devilish behavior. See what I am saying? This is just a footnote.

But, my point is, we have got to come up with mature forms of black self-love, black self-respect in which whiteness is not a point of reference, either negative or positive. Some of the problems I have with certain Afrocentric thinkers is, I think they are too preoccupied with Europe. So Europe has Shakespeare, we have got to come up something. The pyramids!

Shakespeare is just another human being who mastered a particular language. There are masters of Amharic. It is not popular, because Amharic is not a popular language in the States. Why would anybody even question that we have to prove ourselves to white persons? Thank God my family and tradition never, ever incorporated the notion that I had to prove my humanity to anybody. They accepted me on my terms, with all the ugliness and the positiveness that makes me my mama's child. You see what I am saying.

It is that kind of statement that you have to be able to stand on your own two feet. But if you are preoccupied with proving yourself all the time, and that is endemic to a lot of black middle-class folks. They have to prove themselves to white folk. Then they are in trouble. Because it means that white folk are defining whether they are accepted or not. And you might not ever get accepted.

I'm twice as good and you still are not accepting me. I'm three times as good, you still are not accepting me. You ought to give up on that quest and say I am who I am. I do the best I can and I'm going to the grave doing the best I can.

That's it. That's what Charlie Parker did. That's what Miles Davis did. That's what Billie Holiday did, you see. That's what James Cleveland did. That's what black preachers do, at their best. They do their best. That's what Reverend C.L. West did, my grandfather. He stood on his own two feet. He didn't worry about whether white folk was talking about him negative or positive, he was just doing his job and loving the people. See what I am saying? That is the third way out. But that discourse of whiteness and blackness wants to put us in this either/or bag.

I will give you another example, quickly. You know, there is a new book out by Stephen Carter called *Reflections of an Affirmative Action Baby*. And I met Stephen Carter. We were at Yale together. He is a very, very talented brother. Very talented. But throughout the book you see that the fundamental concern is, he has got to be sure that his white peers accept him the way they accept his white colleagues. And he is convinced that affirmative action has gotten in the way of gaining that respect from his white colleagues.

So, therefore, he begins to call affirmative action into question. And I tell Steve, I say what if there is not affirmative action, brother? What if, without affirmative action, you still wouldn't get the respect you want. What are you going to do then?

They didn't respect Du Bois. That was before affirmative action. All that white male mediocrity up at Harvard where Du Bois could have been teaching. They didn't respect him. They wouldn't even publish his text. In retrospect, he is a towering figure. Max Weber said he is one of the most talented sociologists I have ever seen, I have ever read. He published Du Bois in the first issue of his journal, you see.

But Du Bois was saying, look, I am realistic enough to know that America is endemically and chronically racist. That there are some good white folk, but they are nowhere near the majority in relation to issues of race. And that I am going to do the best that I can for all people of goodwill who are willing to join me. And he went on about his work.

Do you see what I am saying? That is what I am talking about. And that is where I think some of the Afrocentrics who are concerned with competing with some of the great European achievements, or some of the assimilationist black folk who are concerned about imitating and aping what they perceive to be white achievements, the white way of life and so on. They both fall through the cracks and miss the best of what I consider to be black culture. But I think this is true for all human beings. Of course, Irish have this vis-a-vis. White Anglo-Saxon Protestants, Jews have this vis-a-vis the goyim, women have this vis-a-vis males, and so on and so forth. So it is a human quest. I think people can learn much from looking at the black plight and predicament and that is why looking at Afro-American studies means that one is never ghettoizing black folk.

But you are recognizing critically their humanity and seeing what can be gained from insights of their humanity for the human species as a whole. And some Americans have actually learned this lesson. That is why jazz is a great contribution of culture in this country.

Pragmatism and the Tragic

Last night I talked about the impact of a market culture and the ways in which the prospect for democracy was called into question by the pervasiveness of market values, market mentality, and market morality. And it may be the case—I think not—but it may be the case that any serious talk about prospects for democracy are empty. That it is too late.

The market fashioning of young people does not provide the kind of critical sensibilities for an active citizenry in a democratic society. Again, for me, this is a challenge, not a conclusion. It raises the question, what are the intellectual and cultural resources of this particular grand, yet in some ways, flawed democratic experiment begun in 1776? Antonio Gramsci—one of the leading cultural theorists of the twentieth century—raised the question, how does one tease out the best of the various traditions that has constituted a civilization?

One of the reasons why I highlight pragmatism is because I am of the opinion that pragmatism is in fact distinctive in the modern world because it is preoccupied with the prospect for democracy, the democratic way of life, as much as a democratic way of governance. And yet, it may indeed be in reflecting upon this tradition, that that which confronts us is overwhelming. And of course, I will be trying to say a word about that this evening [in the final lecture]. About what the future looks like.

So, in sharp contrast to last night, when I was primarily treading in historical waters, I am going to be treading in philosophical waters today. Looking at this very rich tradition of American pragmatism. Noting, as I said last night, that pragmatism has nothing to do with vulgar practicalism, or unprincipled opportunism. It is usually associated with one of those two.

Pragmatism has to do with trying to conceive of knowledge, reality and truth in such a way that it promotes the flowering and flourishing of individuality under conditions of democracy.

The recent revival of pragmatism provides a timely intellectual background for the most urgent problem of our post-modern moment. That is a complex cluster of questions and queries regarding the meaning and value of democracy. No other modern philosophical tradition has grappled with the various dimensions of this problem more than that of American pragmatism. The grand spiritual godfathers of pragmatism, Thomas Jefferson, Ralph Waldo Emerson, Abraham Lincoln, laid the foundation for the meaning and value of democracy in America in the modern world. These foundations consist roughly of, first, the irreducibility of individuality within participatory communities. I will say that again. The irreducibility of individuality within participatory communities.

Second, is the heroic action of ordinary people in a world of radical contingency. And third, is a deep sense of evil that fuels a struggle for justice. The reason that I am preoccupied with a sense of the tragic is that I am preoccupied with our moment in which we must look defeat, disillusionment and discouragement in the face and work through it. A sense of the tragic is an attempt to keep alive some sense of possibility. Some sense of hope. Some sense of agency. Some sense of resistance in a moment of defeat and disillusionment and a moment of discouragement.

Pragmatism, as I shall suggest, has not come to terms with the sense of the tragic and hence we need revisionist understanding of this tradition, even as we build upon the best of it. Now Jeffersonian notions of the irreducibility of individuality within participatory communities is an attempt to sidestep, on the one hand, rapacious individualism, and on the other hand, authoritarian communitarianism. To walk a tightrope between an individualism, hedonism and narcissism in careers, self-centered on the one hand. And on the other hand, conceptions of community that impose values from above, thereby threatening precious liberties.

Jefferson tried to do this by situating unique selves within active networks of power sharing. That protect liberties, that promote prosperity and that highlight accountability. In this sense, Jefferson's ideal combines much of the best of liberalism, of populism and of civic republicanism. And of course, I am talking about the Jefferson who penned the Declaration of Independence, one of the great moral events of the modern period.

We also know Jefferson was a slave-holder, of course, and Jefferson cannot be viewed independently of the critique that David Walker put forward in his classic *Appeal to the Colored Citizens of the World*. A powerful text that must be read alongside Jefferson, because there are long critical readings of Jefferson's *Notes on Virginia* in that famous manifesto.

And he uses Jefferson. He calls Jefferson one of the great philosophers of his day. And he uses Jefferson's own formulations to bring critique to bear on Jefferson's slave holding. Building on the insights of Jefferson as such an exemplary democratic theorist, but then calling into question Jefferson's practice that fell so short of what he was writing about. David Walker in many ways goes hand in hand with Jefferson. But, ironically, David Walker is situated within a Jeffersonian tradition as he critiques Jefferson himself. Because he is furthering the ideals of democracy that Jefferson articulates, even as he brings critique to bear on Jefferson's slave holding.

Emerson's formulations of heroic action of ordinary folk in a world of radical contingency try to jettison static dogmatisms on the one hand, and impersonal determinisms on the other. He attempts to do this by accenting the powers of unique individuals to make and remake themselves with no original models to imitate or emulate. This is so very important. And as I noted last night, I think it is one of the grand breakthroughs of the Age of Europe. This notion of locating human powers and faculties, the capacity to make and remake a self, and society, locating those powers among ordinary people in the commonplace.

This is new. The Greeks had no notion of tragedy as it applied to ordinary people. Most of you know the hierarchy of the Greeks. Tragedy was reserved for the highbrow and the upper class. Only comedy was applicable to ordinary people. Erich Auerbach talks about this in his famous text *Memisis: The Representation of Reality in Western Literature.* It was published in 1941. He says that there is a dark contrast between the Christian tradition in which, in biblical stories, one can capture the grandeur, sublime and tragedy among ordinary people. An ordinary David for example. Ordinary Noah. And yet, the hierarchy of styles holds this at arm's length. This is a profoundly democratic sensibility. The locating of human powers among ordinary people.

Emerson in many ways embodies this. Of course, Abraham Lincoln used to say that God must love common folk because God made so many of them. One of the great democratic artists (distinct from his politics) of our day, Frank Capra, born in Palermo, Italy, and died a few weeks ago, captured this in *It's A Wonderful Life.* One of the greatest films ever made. Not so much technically, but because it crystallized the precious value of an ordinary human being. The uniqueness, the sanctity and the dignity of an ordinary human being who could provide a disclosure of the human condition in the ways in which the Greeks thought only kings were capable of. Even the great Shakespeare confined this quality to the princes of his day. It is profoundly democratic and also we should say, a profoundly American sensibility. Emersonian ideals bring together salutary aspects of romanticism and Protestantism.

Lincoln's profound wrestling with a deep sense of evil that feuls the struggle for justice, endeavors to hold at bay false optimisms and paralyzing pessimisms by positing unique selves that fight other finite opponents rather than demonic foes. This distinction between finite opponents and demonic foes is fundamental. It has to do with my second moment last night. It has to do with the notion of empathy.

In a democratic society, you cannot demonize because demonizing means you have lost contact with the humanity of your foes. You struggle, you take a stand, you fight. But once you demonize, then you are calling into question the possibility of dialogue or further engagement down the line. This is something, of course, that Lincoln understood well. You read that second inaugural lecture closely in the Lincoln Memorial. It says malice toward none, charity toward all. He is talking about Southern opponents. He refuses to demonize, even as they have murdered the sons of the North. It takes a profound sense of statesmanship and a deep understanding of evil to make that distinction.

Of course, Martin Luther King, Jr. understood this well, himself. Bull Connor was never a demonic foe. He was a misguided human being who had racist sensibilities. That realization is part of a great tradition. Lincoln's ideals hold together valuable insights into Christianity and American constitutionalism, which is so very important, and incorporate Scottish commonsensical realism. Yet, interestingly, enough, not one American philosophical thinker has put forward a conception of the meaning of and significance of democracy in light of these foundations laid by Jefferson, Emerson and Lincoln.

If there is one plausible candidate, it would have to be John Dewey. Like Maurice Marterlinck and Walt Whitman. It is very important that in Lincoln's lifetime, Whitman was the only writer to describe Lincoln with love. But Dewey understood that if one takes democracy as an object of philosophical investigation, then one must grapple with the contributions of Jefferson and Emerson. And Dewey wrote some wonderful essays on both figures.

But I suggest that Dewey failed to meet seriously the challenge posed by Lincoln. Namely, he never defined the relation of democratic ways of thought and life to a profound sense of evil. Within the development of post-Dewey pragmatism, only Sidney Hook's suggestive essay, "Pragmatism and the Tragic Sense of Life" responds to Lincoln's challenge in a serious manner. Yet it remained far from the depths of other tragic democratic thinkers like Herman Melville, in my view, the greatest literary artist ever produced in this country. Or F.O. Mathiessen, mid-twentieth century literary critic who was preoccupied with the possibility that America might be unique among modern nations, beginning with a moment of perceived innocence and moving to corruption without a mediating stage of maturity.

That lays bare the problematic of his work. In his *The American Renaissance* of '41, he struggles with this. Or the third, is of course, Reinhold Niebuhr. Especially the Niebuhr of the 30s. There is only one other great American philosopher, and Alfred North Whitehead's origins exclude him in this regard, so I am not including Whitehead. He was born in Britain and didn't come to the States until he was in his 60s, to Harvard. There was only one great American philosopher who seriously grappled with the challenge posed by Lincoln and that is Josiah Royce.

Josiah Royce's name rarely comes up these days. I want to suggest that he is a figure with whom we must grapple and of course, I grapple with him from my vantage point because I am concerned about prospects for democracy. And I am concerned about prospects for democracy because I am concerned about pervasive death and disease and destruction in the country, especially in working poor and very poor communities. But Royce deserves our attention.

I would go so far as to say that Royce's systematic post-Kantian idealism is primarily a long and winding set of profound meditations on the relation of the deep sense of evil to human action, human agency.

Therefore, a contemporary encounter between Dewey

and Royce is not an antiquarian reconstruction of exchanges in the philosophical journals. They had a number of exchanges in the journal *Philosophy and Philosophical Review* and so forth. But that is not what I am after. Nor is it a synoptic synthesis of Dewey's instrumentalism and Royce's idealism. That is not what I am after either. Rather, this encounter is a response to the pressing problem of our day that creatively infuses the contributions of Jefferson, Emerson and Lincoln in our quest for the meaning and value of democracy.

You can imagine that this has profound national implications given the fact that democracy is now on the lips of most of the elites in second world countries that were once part of the Soviet empire. It is on the lips of Gorbachev. It is on the lips of South Africans, so that this struggle with the meaning and value of democracy has global significance.

Royce viewed his project as what he called absolute pragmatism, primarily owing to valuable lessons learned from his close friend William James. The Dewey/Royce encounter is an affair within an American tradition, within the pragmatic tradition. Hence the major philosophic progeny of Jefferson, Emerson and Lincoln carry the banner of American pragmatism.

Let me be very clear about what I mean about pragmatism. There are three principle philosophic slogans of pragmatism: voluntarism; fallibilism; and lastly, experimentalism. I'll define each of those in turn.

Voluntarism, Fallibilism & Experimentalism

Both Royce and Dewey are philosophers of human will, of human power, and human action. By voluntarism, we mean putting a premium on human will, human power and human action. And social practices sit at the center of their distinct philosophic visions. Structured and unstructured, contingent social practices. In short, they agree with the best characterization of pragmatism ever penned, that of C.I. Lewis—Clarence Irving Lewis—when he said that pragmatism could be characterized as the doctrine that all problems are, at bottom, problems of conduct. That all judgments are implicitly judgments of value. And that, as there can be ultimately no valid distinction of theoretical and practical, so there can be no final separation of questions of truth of any kind from questions of the justifiable ends of action.

Dewey's stress on the primacy of human will is shot through all of his major works. His seminal conception of experience as against that of British imperialists and Kantian transcendentalists will suffice for our purposes. It is found in his classic essay penned in 1917. "The Need for a Recovery of Philosophy" says that experience is primarily a process of undergoing, a process of withstanding something. Of passion, of affection in the literal sense of these words. As organisms we're linguistically conscious animals. What linguistically conscious organisms have to endure, to undergo is the consequence of our own actions. Experience, then, is a matter of simultaneous doings and sufferings. Our undergoings are experiments themselves in varying the course of events. Our active tryings are trials and tests of ourselves. This is Dewey in 1917.

Royce also puts the premium on human will and embraces his stress of Dewey. Royce says no truth is a saving truth. Yes, no truth is truth at all unless it guides and directs life. Therefore, he hardily agrees with the current pragmatism and with William James himself. Every opinion expresses an attitude of the will, of preparedness for action. A determination to guide a plan of action in accordance with an ideal.

There is no such thing as a purely intellectual form of assertion which has no element of action about it. An opinion is a deed. It is a deed intended to guide other deeds. It proposes to have what the pragmatists call workings. That is, it undertakes to guide the life of the one who asserts the opinion. In this sense all truth is practical.

Now the voluntaristic impulse of Dewey and Royce leads to two basic notions. First is the notion that truth is a species of the good. This is a very important formulation. Because with the emergence of modern science, the new physics of Newton and the new astronomy of Kepler, and the new probability theory of the Port Royal group, a conception of truth was put forward that was distinct from any conception of the good, because truth had to do with generating high levels of prediction and explanation. And a true theory was one that predicted better, and explained more broadly. And so there was a severing in the seventeenth century, and especially crystallized in the eighteenth century in Europe, between truth-talk and ethics.

So that the notion of truth being a species of the good, is radically called into question. And truth became the providence of the reality claims put forth by the new physicists. So, they would tell us that this table is actually the neutrons and protons bubbling up against one another because by positing those unobservable entities it would provide high levels of prediction. Of course, most of us do believe that those protons, neutrons and electrons are doing precisely what the physicists say they are. Because they do generate high levels of prediction. But it looks like a table to us. Its aesthetic surface is pushed aside, because quantitative myths are now being deployed. And the mathematicization of knowledge, which goes hand in hand with the despiritualization of the natural objects being observed, went hand in hand with the severing from any talk of knowledge and ethics.

Pragmatism comes along and says no. They accept the high levels of prediction of the new priesthood of knowledge, the physicists. They believe that the physicists are in fact engaged in very important activities that generate human control and mastery over nature. But they refuse to provide that new priesthood of knowledge with a monopoly on truth. They simply provide the highest level of prediction and explanation. It is a very crucial move. Truth is a species of the good.

Second, that the conception of the good is defined in relation to temporal consequences. This is very important as well because, as we shall see, it puts a premium on the future, and for the first time in modern philosophy there would be a tradition that would be obsessed with looking forward rather than looking backward. Philosophical traditions have been preoccupied with representing. That is what representation is. Providing copies of that which happened in the past. Representations of that which happened in the past. To recapture, to recuperate that which happened in the past. But pragmatism says no. Truth is a species of the good and the conception of the good has to do with defining it in relation to temporal consequences prospectively.

The first notion of the truth as a species of the good means that our beliefs about the way the world is have ethical significance. William James writes that our opinions about the nature of things belong to our moral life. That is a profound point. If you believe that natural objects are solely what quantitative models say they are, then your conception of who you are as a human being means that you are simply a body in space,

to be explained and predicted. Your loves, your cares, your anxieties, your frustrations, that is very much like the aesthetic surface of this table. It is pushed aside. But there is a fundamental link between what you understand the nature of reality to be and your conception of yourself as a human being. Again, ethics and epistemic claims go hand-in-hand.

Dewey himself, I think, captures this best when he says that philosophy is a form of desire, an effort or action of love, namely of wisdom, but we add as a proviso not attached to the platonic use of the word, that wisdom, whatever it is, is not a mode of science or knowledge. Philosophy which was conscious of its own business and province would then perceive that it is an intellectualized wish. An aspiration subjected to rational discrimination and tests. A social hope reduced to a working program of action. A prophecy of the future, but one disciplined by serious thought and knowledge. Philosophy is a quest for wisdom. A wisdom is not reducible to knowledge. It is not a trashing of knowledge. We must avoid the situating of knowledge that falls short of wisdom.

Royce chimes in on the same theme. He says opinions about the universe are counsels as to how to adjust your deeds to the purposes and requirements which are a survey of the whole of one's life.

This notion of truth as a species of the good is to define the good in relation to temporal consequences, meaning that the future has ethical significance. And actually, if there is a distinctive feature of pragmatism, it is precisely this notion. That the future has ethical significance. Its emphasis on the ethical significance of the future provides pragmatism with a new way of talking about possibility and potentiality of human organisms.

Dewey, I think, captures this best in his 1922 essay entitled "The Development of American Pragmatism" where he says, pragmatism presents itself with an extension of historical empiricism, but with a fundamental difference. It does not insist upon antecedent phenomena, but on consequent phenomena. Not upon the precedence, but on the possibilities of action. This change in point of view is almost revolutionary, he says, in its consequences for the history of philosophy. An empiricism which is content with repeating facts already past, has no place for possibility and for liberty. Pragmatism thus has a metaphysical implication.

The doctrine of the value of consequences leads us to take the future into consideration and this takes us to the conception of a universe whose evolution is not finished, of a universe which is still, in James's term, "in the making." In the process of becoming. Up to a certain point, still plastic. For pragmatism, in the future has ethical significance because human will, human thought, and action can make a difference in relation to human aims and purposes. There is moral substance in the fact that human will can make the future different and possibly better. This preoccupation with the perspective leads Dewey to quip, "what should experience be but a future implicated in a present?"

Based on what I presented last night, I hope we can begin to see what happens in our moment when a distinctive philosophical tradition of this country that puts such a premium on the future clashes with the breakdown in social systems of nurturing children in which their conception of the future narrows, hollows, and hence a moment in a very unique civilization and culture, in which the possibility, the sense of possibility, is more and more called into question.

My query, of course, is whether in fact, looking at this distinct philosophical tradition, there are ways of teasing out some resources that can speak to our moment. To sustain some sense of possibility, some sense of a different and better future. And this is why the sense of the tragic becomes very important for me because we have to recognize the degree to which the sense of defeat and disillusionment is quite real indeed. This makes important Jefferson's notions of periodic revolutions, of course, that one finds in the Declaration of Independence, every generation or two, people's accountability should be enacted by radically changing American government. It is one of those moments in the Declaration of Independence that people aren't comfortable with. They say, Jefferson, you had your revolution, that is enough. Jefferson says no, we need to be cleansing. I think it upset people in 1969 that the Black Panthers used to sit in front of state capitals and read that portion of the Declaration of Independence. I saw Huey Newton read it himself when he was released from jail. And people would say what revolutionary doctrine is he reading now. It is Jefferson's Declaration of Independence.

Similar to this is Emerson's talk about onward transitions and upward crossings. Everything good is on the highway, Emerson would say. The pragmatist's emphasis on the future terrain for humans making a difference results in a full-blown fallibilism and experimentalism. All facts are fallible, all experience is experimental.

This is the common ground of pragmatism upon which both Dewey and Royce stand. Unique selves acting in and through participatory communities give ethical significance to an open, risk-ridden future. The slogans are, then, of voluntarism, fallibilism in which every claim is open to revision. And experimentalism, calling into question any form of dogmatism, orthodoxy is criticism and self-correction. It is a central component of any human enterprise.

The majesty of community goes hand in hand with what Royce called the true spirituality of genuine doubting. Nothing blocks the road to inquiry. That the road to inquiry is open to all travelers to the degree to which they are willing to allow their relative ignorance or naked power to be put in the spotlight. Yet, Dewey and Royce part company in response to Lincoln's challenge. A deep sense of evil affects Royce more than it does Dewey. In fact, Royce clings to his post-Kantian idealism, even after his appropriation of Peirce's theory of interpretive communities, owing to his philosophic grappling with suffering and sorrow.

Jamesian injunctions about the strenuous move against evil did not suffice for Royce. Nor Dewey's leaps of faith in critical intelligence. Royce holds on to his Christian-like dramatic portrait of reality with his hope for and assurance of ultimate triumph precisely because his sense of evil and his sense of the tragic is so deep.

What separates Royce from other American pragmatists and most American philosophers, though Adorno is the only present day philosopher who comes to mind here, is Royce's prolonged and poignant engagement with the thought of Arthur Schopenhauer. Arthur Schopenhauer is a name that is rarely talked about in America, and maybe less so in Tulsa. Given the evangelical zeal of this particular area of the country. Arthur Schopenhauer is not simply a footnote prior to Friederich Nietzsche.

But he is a profound philosopher of pessimism with elected affinities to Buddhism and he serves for Royce as a major challenge concerning how one talks about pervasive suffering and sorrow and human life. Royce's response to Lincoln's challenge takes the form of a lifelong struggle with pessimism.

The first course that Royce ever taught in the United States was taught on Arthur. Very un-American, given the land of idealism and optimism. The first graduate course ever taught in America was on Schopenhauer, 1877, and of course, at Johns Hopkins, the first research institution in this country. His classic text, *The Spirit of Modern Philosophy* published in 1892 contains 33 pages on Kant, 28 on Fichte, 37 on Hegel and 36 pages on Schopenhauer.

This is an atypical history of modern philosophy. Most modern philosophers spend 80 pages on Kant and 3 pages on Schopenhauer. I know of no other history of modern philosophy where Schopenhauer's treated so extensively and respectfully. For Royce, Schopenhauer is, and I quote, "a great thinker, significant. A philosopher of considerable dignity. Equipped with an erudition vast rather than technical." That is a wonderful phrase. Erudition vast rather than technical. "Enjoyed manifold labors rather than professional completeness." Wonderful phrases here.

Royce states that Schopenhauer's principal work, *The World As Will and Representation* is the most artistic philosophical treatise in existence, with the exception of Plato's dialogues. This is a kind of praise that Royce provides and gives Schopenhauer. Furthermore, Schopenhauer is a further transition of figure from the romantic idealism to the modern realism. In every major text of Royce, including his lectures on modern idealism, published posthumously, Schopenhauer makes a significant appearance.

In short contrast, Schopenhauer, along with Lincoln's challenge of a deep sense of evil in the tragic makes no appearances in Dewey's volumes. No Schopenhauer. This is where I find Royce profound and poignant, while I find Dewey sane, fascinating, but unsatisfactory. Like Melville, Matthiessen and Niebuhr, I believe a deep sense of evil in the tragic must inform the meaning and value of democracy.

The culture of democratic societies require not only civic virtues of participation, tolerance, openness, mutual respect and mobility. But also dramatic struggles with the two major culprits, death and disease, that cut-off the joys of democratic citizenship. Such citizenship must not be so preoccupied or obsessed with possibility that it conceals and represses the ultimate facts of the human predicament. This is neither the time nor place to plunge into Royce's rich reflections on evil.

I recommend his 1897 essay, "The Problem of Job," which in many ways exceeds that of his classic essay "The Practical Significance of Pessimism" that he wrote in 1879, but instead, just very briefly, I will end by saying something about his notion of irrevocable deeds as a source of his conception of the absolute in his most straightforward book, *Sources of Religious* insight, he published in 1912. Royce introduces this notion in the midst of a complimentary discussion of pragmatism.

He says, one of the central facts about life is that every deed one does is *ipso facto* irrevocable. That is, at any moment you perform a given deed, you cannot deny it. If you perform it, it is done and cannot be undone. This difference between what is done and what is undone is, in the real and empirical world, a perfectly absolute difference. The opportunity for a given individual deed returns not, for the moment that that individual deed can be done, nothing recurs. Here is a case where the rational constitution of the whole universe gets into definite relation to our momentary experience. And if anyone wants to be in touch with the absolute, with that reality which the pragmatists fancy to be peculiarly remote in abstract, let him or her simply try to undo that deed.

This is very important, because Royce's notion of the absolute has been associated with floating in platonic skies with forms and so forth. But we say no. The absolute actually is the most practical, tangible, on-the-ground reality. Let the experience teach him or her what one means by calling reality absolute. Let the truth which that experience teaches any rational being show them what is meant by absolute truth. Now Royce's point here is not simply to draw attention to the limits that the past imposes on the future, because keep in mind what is distinctive about pragmatism is the premium on the future, the sense of possibility, potentiality as we see it.

And Royce wants to affirm this as do I. But he also wants to talk about the pastness in the present. And the way in which the pastness in the present does impose constraints on the future and here, of course, he echoes that famous essay of 1919, of Thomas Stearns Eliot, "Tradition and the Individual Talent." Where he talks about the past and of the present. He talks about how, in fact, tradition is something you don't inherit. It is something you gain by great labor, you see. A fairly Eliotic moment in Royce's formulation here. Royce is trying to show just how concrete and practical the notion of the absolute or the weight of the past can be.

His aim is to unhinge notions of the absolute from their association with the unpractical and the inaccessible. He wants to better enable unique selves to act in the present and give ethical significance to the future by providing standards that transcend the present. Royce recognizes there must be some notions of standards with regulative and critical force, though always partial and fragmentary, which sustain our strenuous mood and the perennial fight against what he calls the capricious, irrationality of the world and the blind irrationality of fortune.

He defends his version of the absolute because he looks to the truth for aid in that battle. On the one hand, he accepts the interplay of what he calls the no longer and the not yet, of the past and the future. Not just a stress on the not yet, but also the no longer, so that fulfillment never at one present instance is to be found. Like Hegel's unhappy consciousness, dissatisfaction reigns and temporal peace is a contradiction in terms. Yet, he is ready to accept the deep sorrow of possessing ideals and taking his share of the divine task. In this way, he defines absolute reality. The sort of reality that belongs to irrevocable deeds. Absolute truth, the sort of truth that belongs to those opinions which for a given purpose counsel individual deeds when the deed in fact meets the purpose for which they were intended. These two are not remote affairs invented by philosophers for the sake of barren intellectualism. Of course, that is a term from William James.

Such absolute reality and absolute truth are the most concrete and practical and familiar of matters. The pragmatist who denies that there is any absolute truth accessible, has never rightly considered the very most characteristic feature of the reasonable wheel, namely that it is always counseling irrevocable deeds and therefore is always giving counsel that is for its own determinate purpose irrevocably right or wrong precisely and insofar as it is definite counsel.

Now what I suggest is that something deeper is going on. That Royce believes more is at stake in warding off subjectivism and relativism than the pragmatists admit. That reality and truth must be in some sense absolute, not only because skepticism lurks about, but also and more importantly because it is the last and only hope for giving meaning to the strenuous mood for justifying the worthwhileness of our struggle to endure. For Royce, James' promotions for heroic action, Emersonian claims at heroic action in and of themselves, are insufficient or Sisyphysian, pushing a rock up a hill, but no progress, unless there is a deeper struggle with the sense of the tragic. One of the great moments in Royce's corpus, a moment not to be found in Dewey is when Royce questions his idealist response to the problem of evil. After pushing pessimism to the brink, struggling with Schopenhauer, like Daniel with the angels, he holds on for dear life. And he says, I do not feel that I have yet quite expressed in full force of the deepest argument for pessimism.

The full seriousness of the problem of evil. Pessimism in the pure sense isn't the doctrine of the merely peevish man, but of the man who, to borrow a word of Hegel's, has once feared not for this or that moment in his life, but who has feared for all of his nature. So that he has trembled through and through and all that was most fixed in him has become shaken. There are experiences in life that do just this for us.

When the foundations of the great deep are once thus broken up and floods have come, it isn't over this or that loss of our green earth that we sorrow. It is because of all that endless waste of tossing waves which now row cubits deep above the top of what were our highest mountains. No, the worst tragedy of the world is the tragedy of brute chance to which everything spiritual seems to subject against us. The tragedy of the diabolical irrationale of the so many among the folds, of whatever is significant.

An open enemy you can face, he says, but the temptation to do evil is indeed the necessity for spirituality. But one's own foolishness, one's ignorance, the cruel accidents of disease, the fatal misunderstandings that part friends and lovers, the chance mistakes that wreck nations. These things we lament most bitterly, not because they are painful, but because they are farcical, distracting.

Not full men worthy of the sword of the spirit, nor yet mere pains of our finitude that we can easily learn to face courageously as one can be indifferent to physical pain. No, he says. These things do not make life merely painful to us, they make it hideously petty. He has gone as far as he can go.

At this point, he seems virtually to throw up his hands and throw in the towel. Fresh memories of his own nervous breakdown only three years earlier, which led him on a trip to Australia, loom large. He concludes, from our own finite point of view, there is no remotely discoverable justification for this caprice.

Yet, he refuses to give in to Schopenhauer and holds that we must dare to hope for an answer. Were our insight into the truth of *logos* based upon a sort of emperical assurance, it would surely fail us here. But not, as it is, if we have the true insight of deeper idealism, we can turn from our chaos to him the suffering God, who in our flesh bears the sins of the world and whose natural body is pierced by the capricious wounds that hateful fools inflict upon him. It is this thought, Royce says, that traditional Christianity has in its deep symbolism first taught the world that in its fullness only an idealistic interpretation can really and rationally express.

What in time is hopelessly lost, is attained for the suffering God in his eternity. We have found in a world of doubt but one assurance. Only one and yet how rich. All else is hypothesis. Royce's leap of faith. Evidence under-determined. The only option to Schopenhauerian pessimism.

I quote at length to convey Royce's response to Lincoln's challenge through Schopenhauer. The point here is not to raise a deeper question as to whether his argument is actually persuasive. That is the subject for a different lecture. Whether this argument is convincing, whether his appropriation of Christianity is persuasive, but rather to highlight the depth of Royce's efforts to sustain some sense of possibility. The strenuous mood in the face of the deep sense of evil.

Never in the tradition of American pragmatism has Lincoln's challenge been taken so seriously. Yet, the democratic legacy in our time of Jefferson, Emerson and Lincoln in our ghastly century, millions gone, dead, burned, murdered, maimed. The democratic legacy demands nothing less so that the encounter between Dewey and Royce may help us preserve the ethical significance of the future of our children.

And tonight, I will be reflecting on what that future may look like in light of the discernment put forward yesterday and in light of Royce's grappling with the philosophical tradition preoccupied with democracy and whether it can speak to the depths of the tragic that we now live and face in our own time. Thank you so very much.

Responses to Questions

(The questions were inaudible on the tape; only the answers are available.)

West: The pragmatist conception of human beings is one of an organism whose faculties are integrated, who is interacting and transacting with an environment. So that when you talk about truth, you are talking about the consensus forged by human beings who agree upon certain common ends and aims. And that consensus forged is a dynamic consensus because nothing blocks the road to inquiry. All claims are in no way immune to revision.

Therefore, truth talk for Dewey, the truth was actually what was warranted assertable at a particular moment that would change over time. I think Richard Rory and others, especially Hilary Putnam, have shown this to be quite unconvincing. The truth is something very different than warranted assertability. But warranted assertability is the best thing that finite human beings do at any particular moment.

And you accept the best truth available at the time, in the same way that 50 years from now we may discover that there is no such thing as electrons and neutrons and Brownian motion is linked to something else. Then we will rewrite all the textbooks, all those years that we believed in protons and neutrons, we just believed the best available theory.

Now, if we accept that notion, then truth talk becomes part of the conditions under which particular communities do forge assertable claims, with values such as appeal to evidence. Publicity of arguments. A whole host of other values. Tolerance, ability, mediating, dialogue and so on. And then the question becomes, what are the aims of these particular communities?

When I talked about the physicist, it is very clear that for them what is at stake is a high level prediction. If somebody presented to the physicist a grand theory that was true, that didn't explain or predict anything, they would say you don't understand our game that we are playing. You have missed the point. A true theory is one that predicts. I have got a true theory, but it doesn't predict anything. No tenure in this department. You missed the point. Because the end and aim, the conception of the good that regulates that community is that prediction is of paramount importance. Explanation is of paramount importance. That is what we are after. Why? Because through prediction and explanation, it leads toward the expansion of human powers over nature.

And that is what is of primary importance. Once you call that into question, then they figure you must be part of a different community. Well, I am not interested in human control over nature. Well, you are in the wrong department. You should be somewhere else. You see that is a certain conception of the good which is surreptitiously tucked away in the truth talk of that community. And of course, pragmatists want to make that visible. If there are other conceptions of the good, there are going to be other kinds of focuses, as with meaning and value of life, for example, in which high levels of prediction aren't helpful to us.

Question.

West: I appreciate that question you asked because it takes us right to the center of the dialogue between various postmodern theorists, who would want to put forth a social constructivist thesis and pragmatists, who themselves claim to endorse social constructiveness thesis, but do not render in their own writings a consciousness of the degree to which they are deploying terms which themselves are constructs.

Now, see, I would opt for the latter. That is to say that

I would opt for the pragmatist who does in fact affirm social constructs from culture to culture, civilization to civilization. It is a historical claim about sheer historical contingency and the way in which various notions, and rubrics and metaphors and what-have-you are always constructs. But in saying they are always constructs, it in no way denies that these constructs themselves are strong enough in the same way that when Royce talks about irrevocable deeds, there is a sheer facticity which is constructed, but is constructed in such a way that it appears natural.

Why? Because it is so unavoidable given the kind of socialization and acculturation human beings undergo in a particular culture. So, we can accent the constructive character of individual deed and whathaveyou. Once we have done that, I am not sure we have done as much as various postmodern theorists think we have done. That is the beginning it seems to me. Do you see what I am saying?

And once pragmatists embrace that, the question still becomes then how do we analyze, discern, respond, overcome, the very constructs that have such a tremendous weight in gravity within the various cultures, in this case, our own culture?

Question.

West: I think that you are onto something very important. And I think that it has to do with the ambivalent character of pragmatism vis-a-vis American market culture. That pragmatism emerges in a culture that is more thoroughly market driven and commodified than any other culture in the modern period. Therefore, you are going to find elective affinities. A stress on mobility, fluidity, border crossing, transgression, calling authority into question. That is what markets do, that is what pragmatism does. The difference, though, I think is that for pragmatism, I think they are trying to present what they view to be the best of that market culture, which are precisely those non-market values such as community which are central going back to Peirce.

Pragmatism and the Tragic

But not just community, but as you know, love. The Agapish of Peirce is all about an evolutionary love. And that love was something that was irreducible to market culture, even as the pragmatism has elective affinities to the market culture, you see.

And part of the problem that we are going to have, and this is so true for prophetic thought, is how does one extract certain elements from market culture while working through market culture and still bring a critique of market culture? Because the market culture has much to teach us in a positive way just as it has a negative way.

That is part of the grappling that is going on here. So I think you are absolutely right. There are deep elective affinities and in fact when you look at pragmatism from outside of a U.S. context, it looks as if pragmatism is nothing but a justification of a market culture. I mean the great Bertrand Russell would say over and over again, pragmatism is just a justification for American commercialism. He was absolutely wrong, he never got the point. But it is understandable from Britain. Because he sees this mobility and fluidity. We are not talking about absolute truth, and so forth and so on. Because none of those terms sound like the market. Pragmatism, on the other hand, looks like commercialism and so forth. Because there were elective affinities, he was not careful and cautious enough to see that Peirce and James were using a language that looked very much like the market when James talks about the cash value of truth. For Russell that is all market talk.

Well, yes and no, Russell. You see it is an appropriation of a commercial metaphor in order to ultimately as we know in James's case of bringing critique to bear upon what he viewed to be some of the pernicious effects of a market culture. Just as he could also observe some of the positive elements of a market culture. So it is that kind of complexity and subtlety that we have to be after in talking about pragmatism's relation to this hotel civilization or business civilization, a market civilization. I will try to talk about that tonight. Any other questions or queries?

Question.

West: Well it is a critique in the interest of revisioning the pragmatism because I do still want to talk about the future and the sense of possibility and so forth. But I do not think that the last option that you put forth, Michael, is actually historically possible. That is to say, when you claim that postmodernists think that somehow they can view the past as just a construct and simply by means of an interpretation, choose which one will have weight or not. That to me is historically impossible. It might be an illusion of intellectuals, but it is historically impossible because of these constructs.

We are talking about the blackness/whiteness discourse in American history, right? That you can talk about it as a construct, but it has been institutionalized, it has been socialized over time so it has a weight or gravity. So on the one hand we know that whiteness and blackness are constructs. But when we talk about the weight of constructs, you see, there is no escape. They are elastic enough to be changed, but you simply don't push it aside by one interpretation. And only a deluded, isolated, ahistorical postmodernist view would argue that that can be done.

It is historically impossible. But I think you are certainly right to say that my concern is trying to keep alive what I called yesterday a nuance historical sense, which is to say, keep alive traditions of critique and resistance, and the use of tradition there is quite deliberate. This is why I invoked Eliot. Eliot had a different concept of the tradition in terms of which one keeps alive. Mine are much more related to the underside of history and the unsaid in history.

He highlights those who tend to be near the top. But there is still much to learn from Thomas Stearns Eliot in terms of how you talk about the relation of past or present. That is what I am preoccupied with. Like Raymond Williams, I think, in *Modern Tragedy*, he is also preoccupied with this from a different vantage point than Eliot politically, but still concerned with the relation of past and present.

And I think you are absolutely right that my critique of pragmatism is an attempt to criticize the way it talks about tradition. Dynamic conceptions of tradition. And traditions that are waning which serve as a springboard for prophetic thought and action given market culture which effaces the past. Undermines traditions and so forth. So that I am in a bind, but rightfully so, there is no escape from dealing with this pragmatist market culture on the one hand and an attempt to recover tradition on the other hand. And thereby, in conversation with people who have talked about traditions in various ways, we see what one can learn from them and then using whatever insights I have to keep alive a tradition of critique and resistance in our present moment.

Question.

West: I think there is a number of different levels on which to respond to that very important question. At the intellectual level in terms of the battle over ideas, we have got to go back and re-examine those exemplary democratic thinkers and figures to evaluate and assess what went into what they thought about democracy.

And I think that links between democracy and humility are very important here, for example at the level of individual living. Because humility is a form of self-criticism that I mentioned before. Self-criticism and self-correction sits at the very center of any human enterprise for pragmatism. But to reconstruct the democratic tradition from past to present, to see what insights we can bring intellectually, that means rereading Walt Whitman closely. He is one of the few democrats of the nineteenth century. Dewey, Du Bois, in our own time Ella Baker, Fanny Lou Hamer, Martin Luther King, Jr., Dorothy Day, Michael Harrington. There is a whole host of persons who are radically democratic individuals as well as fighters for democracy.

And this has been a problem with the Left, because the

Left has always been ambivalent about democratic values. Promoting it at certain times, rejecting it under elitist values at other times. Managerial politics under Leninist auspices, and then pro-democratic sensibilities under democratic socialist auspices. So there is a real ambivalence on the Left. The Right has been quite explicit about what it thinks about democracy: As little as possible, as little as one can get away with. Reform bills in Britain in 1832, 1867, 1887. Look at some of the discussions that go along with the expansion of democracy and what very subtle and sophisticated right wing intellectuals have to say about it. Look at the debate between Walter Lippmann and John Dewey in the 1920s, when Lippmann wrote a book called *The Phantom Public*, and another book called *Public Opinion*. And Dewey responded with *The Public and Its Problems*.

Lippmann's argument was, I once was a democrat, but I have given up on it because I don't think ordinary people can do anything right. I vest my faith in those elites who can at least guide society through its crises. Common folk are simply gullible to irrational symbols. I don't think they have the capacity for self-government any more. Abe Lincoln would turn over in his grave. Abe Lincoln had said self-government is better than good government. That's Lincoln. What did he mean? Well, the good Alexander II of Russia was a good government. He died. Alexander III came in and all hell broke loose. Why? Because there was no check. No check. No accountability. So you might have good government for a moment because you have a nice benevolent despot or what-have-you. Then he or she dies and boom, you have another malevolent despot. Self-government, always messy, difficult, compromising and so forth, but it is on a democratic track. And that is precisely in part what Dewey said to Lippmann and his book. He said the cure for the ills of democracy is more democracy. Of course, this is so very important for people below.

You remember Malcolm X's technical definition of a black person, of a nigger. He said a nigger is a victim of

Pragmatism and the Tragic

American democracy. That was his formulation. It is oxymoronic. How can there be victims of American democracy? Well, there have been. Jeffersonian democracy: black folk pushed further back; slavery consolidated. Poor whites in the South move to the center. Jim Crow. On two different tracks democracy is expanding for certain folk, curtailed for others. And yet, the irony is only more democracy would enhance the plight of victims of American democracy.

Malcolm understood that. King did. Ella Baker did as well. And hence, how do we talk about this tradition of democracy? And it gets, as you can imagine, quite complex. Because most democracies that we know have been predicated on empire or imperialism. From the Greeks to the Brits and the United States where democracy is predicated on slavery. What does it mean to talk about democracy in a world in which colonies are gone for the most part?

The empire is still here in economic form, but colonies are gone. And slavery for the most part is gone. That is what I mean by prospects of democracy. It is very difficult to talk seriously about this. There is a wonderful book out by Eli Sagan called *On Democracy and Paranoia in Greece and America*. Precious honey and deadly hemlock. And democracy has both at the same time.

This is one of the interventions presently in terms of struggling with this issue of what we mean by democracy. I think a tradition that we ought to be rereading is a tradition of British new liberals. A tradition of John Morley, the old radical independent, L.T. Hobhouse, J.A. Hobson, C.P. Clark and others at the turn of the century who were concerned about severing democratic forms of liberalism from British forms of imperialism.

It fundamentally shapes around the Boer War in the 1890s. There is a wonderful book by Hobhouse called *Democracy and Reaction* which ought to be read by every American citizen, not because it is right, but because it has some insight. Most libraries don't even have the book but it was published in 1903 and it is fascinating, in fact.

In this book—in the same year Du Bois was talking about the problem of the twentieth century, the problem of the color line—Hobhouse says that the problem of the twentieth century will be the relation of democracy to white racial domination and the women's struggle. In 1903, 1904, come on Hobhouse, how did you get it right, partly at least?

He is trying to rethink the notion of democracy and he is a liberal, but he can't go with Chamberlain and the other pro-imperialists. He has to rethink democracy in relation to race and empire and gender and so on. I know it is getting late and we need to go eat lunch. Thank you so very much for coming in today.

The Future of Pragmatic Thought

When talking about the future of prophetic thought, you recall last night, I began by highlighting those four fundamental components: human discernment, human connection, human hypocrisy and human hope. I would think that if I can leave you with any sense of hope, convince myself that the hope that I have is not a delusion in our present times, then I would have made some contribution. I also want to acknowledge the degree to which any reflection about human hope has as much to do with the battle of ideas as it does the battle for resources. So the first thesis I want to put forward is that the future of prophetic thought depends on our capacity to preserve, cultivate and expand traditions of critique and resistance. These have to do with trying to deepen those four components that I talked about last night.

Human discernment is in a very very deep and profound intellectual crisis of our time, that has much to do with what we mean by freedom. What do we mean by democracy and what are the prospects of freedom and democracy? That is one of the reasons why I highlighted the pragmatic tradition this afternoon. Because without a serious intellectual reflection about what we mean by these precious terms, much of our energy will be spent in our struggles for freedom and our struggles for democracy without a clear meaning of what we have in mind.

I am going to be using as a case study black America tonight because it seems to me any serious reflection about the possibilities for expanding freedom and democracy in the USA have to do with coming to terms with this hard case. These people of African descent, many of whom have been here nine generations—it is the best of times and the worst of times for black America. The best of times for those who now have access to unprecedented opportunities, making their quick entre into the middle classes. And the worst of times for 31 percent who still live in dire poverty and violence ridden conditions with very little access to resources. Very little sense of self that could project over time and space, locked into a market culture in the buying and selling of drugs and bodies. And then there is the majority of people of African descent. The people who are usually overlooked are the hard working-class black men and women, attempting to make ends meet and preserve their sense of dignity and decency. The future of prophetic thought and action depends in part on the capacity of prophetic traditions to remain alive, especially among those persons on the underside of our society. But not solely, by any stretch of the imagination, on the underside.

Before focusing on black America, I think we have to begin with the various traditions that would help us analyze what it means to be a product of American culture. I want to suggest that there are two distinctive features of American civilization. The first is a sacred cow of this civilization: economic growth by means of corporate priorities. Let me say that again—economic growth by means of corporate priorities. Calvin Coolidge said the business of America is business. I would add that the business of America has been primarily big business, from agribusiness to transnational corporations. And those who call into question economic growth by means of corporate priorities are always already going against the grain because they are calling for the redistribution of wealth and power in the United States. The society in which 1 percent of the population owns 30 percent of the wealth—not income I'm talking about but wealth—the properties, the stock, the dividends. Another way of looking at this is that the bottom 45 percent of the population own 2 percent of the wealth.

So the first distinctive feature is this sacred cow, which makes America a very conservative society even given its

The Future of Pragmatic Thought

dynamic economy. This corporate sector and this entrepreneurial sector—our economy—is a relatively fluid social structure, giving the possibility of social mobility for those who are prepared—for those who have accessed education and skills. Yet the distribution of wealth and power is rarely questioned. I think I made the point last night that in the 1960s one of the reasons why American society was much more open to including those who had been systematically excluded was because the economy was expanding so quickly. There was less to give up. But after '73 the contraction began. So the first feature is this commitment to economic growth—corporate power.

The second is that we live in a society which is chronically and endemically racist, patriarchal and homophobic. What I mean by that is not that America has any monopoly on evil. Most societies that we know are chronically xenophobic in some way. But America has its distinctive form of it. I talked a bit about it last night in terms of discourse of whiteness and blackness. Discourseness of maleness and femaleness. Most societies we know in human history has been patriarchal. The tragic plight of women through time and space. America has its own distinctive forms of sexism and patriarchy. And similarly so in terms of homophobia. But the point I want to make here is that those who will be explicitly open about their anti-racist and anti-sexist stands will be cutting against the grain. Cutting against the grain— that's the tradition of critique and resistance to racism. The critiques and resistance to sexism. Cutting against the grain. It means, then, that there is not a broad terrain upon which to work in a society that views it as relatively taboo to call for redistribution of wealth and power from top to bottom. Or relatively taboo about highlighting deeply xenophobic practices. And when we look at American history we see the prophetic and progressive traditions to be very, very marginal indeed. Not that they haven't made a difference. But there is so much to give up, given all the comfort and convenience that the skilled in such a privileged country can have access to, why would anyone want to give it up as opposed to struggling against the maldistribution of wealth? Endemic racism and sexism and homophobia—you see.

We look at the 1890s and the grand populist movement—farmers had been pushed out. Workers beginning to organize against overwhelming odds. Look at the Pullman strike of 1894 in Chicago. Crushed and/or absorbed by prevailing political parties. In the 1930s, CIO—the drive to organize semiskilled and unskilled workers, to attempt interracial struggle as did the early populists, you see. Crushed or absorbed by one of the major political parties. In the 1960s came the new wave of social motion and social momentum and social movement. Crushed and/or absorbed by one of the major political parties. The best that the prophetic tradition has been able to do on the American terrain is to generate social motion and to produce a social movement. But every social movement was either crushed or absorbed. This is why it takes a tremendous act of faith, in the long run a tremendous act of courage to cut against the American grain in a serious way. Because the powers that be are serious about their entrenched interests.

Take the Christian tradition. We saw the social gospel movement along with the populist and the progressive movement at the turn of the century. In the 1930s we saw trade union Christians siding with the workers. In the 1960s we saw Christians engaging in anti-racist struggle. First from Martin Luther King, Jr. and later with various black power advocates. In each instance, the Christians call forth to plunge to the depth of their understanding of the Christian gospel and to believe that it has something to do with the dignity and sanctity of each and every individual including working people, including farmers, including black people, including women. But always a minority. Now it doesn't mean that we demonize the majority. It simply means that the majority chooses to go with the mainstream because it is easier. And what we have to do is to reflect on what the conditions are for the possibility of the next wave of social motion and social movement.

I must say in all candor that my understanding of my own calling as a freedom fighter in the black Christian tradition is to devote time and energy to doing all that I can to generate the new wave of social action. And it will not be a wave that is confined solely to electoral politics. It will be extra-parliamentary, which is to say it will take forms of action within and outside of electoral politics.

For me, then, the future of prophetic thought has to do with the future of social movements and social motion that could bring power and pressure to bear on the present-day status quo. International outlook but local bases. What are the ideals that regulate such action? First, it is a profoundly democratic ideal that says that ordinary people ought to be able to participate in the decision-making processes and institutions that guide and regulate their lives.

But democracy itself is still a means. And it is a means for the flowering of individuality. Why do I see it this way? Because I stand fundamentally on the profoundly Christian notion that we are each made equal in the eyes of God. That Rockefeller has the same status as a peasant in Alabama. And that peasant in Alabama has the same right to human flourishing as any other human being regardless of race, regardless of religion, regardless of nation, regardless of gender. It is a deep, spiritually-based notion of equality. Doesn't mean that we have the same natural capacities. Doesn't mean that we have the same natural talents. But we ought to have the same opportunities. We ought to have the same chances.

These sound like elementary formulations and in many ways they are. But if you follow them seriously, they will pit you against the grain. Against every set of power elite in every society I know. When democracy is taken seriously with its end of individuality to flourish and flower, it makes every set of elites tremble in their boots. Right across the board—Russia, Kenya, India, Brazil, Costa

Rica or the United States.

If one takes these ideals seriously it means one is a radical democrat, small d. It doesn't mean that democracy is your religion. It means that democracy is entailed by your Christian faith. It is part of your ethical obligation to fight for as a Christian who takes seriously the equal status of individuals. Radical democracy means that there must be relative access to resources for these unique individuals. And the resources I have in mind are first and foremost basic social goods. Food, clothing, shelter, education, employment, childcare, health care. And that these basic social goods must be provided by the common fare of the public sphere. They are not subject to market mechanisms.

Of course in this society, the only such good tends to be water which is free, at least in some places. And a lot of water fountains don't work in New York. I don't know what it is like in Tulsa. Doesn't mean you call into question market mechanisms per se. Market mechanisms have proven to be indispensable for both preservation of liberties and generating levels of productivity such that there is wealth to be distributed. But basic social goods ought not be subject to market mechanisms. Of course we know the history of this struggle. 100 years ago, children were still working 16 hours a day in work places, unprotected. Why? Because the labor movement was weak or that black and white tenant farmers were locked into debt bondage, because the farmer's movement was weak. Or that women were locked into domestic space so that their potential was constrained, because the woman's movement was weak.

It has been a long and hard struggle of people who have given their time, their energy, their blood, and their lives to provide some space over against the powers that would exploit their labor, that would degrade their character. The 40-hour work week is only 51 years old. It was enacted in 1940. Only by a labor struggle. Black people pushing back the apartheid-like rule of law—in place 80 years. Only because courageous men and women—prophetic men and women of all races but disproportionately Black folk—decided to straighten up their backs and either die or win in the fight for freedom. This was a hard thing to ask of anybody. And especially an oppressed people, because they are preoccupied with survival rather than the struggle for freedom. They are thinking about the next day and the next week and the next month rather than some vision of emancipation. But when they decide to straighten their backs up again, there is going to be a camp meeting in the USA in every major urban center. And that camp meeting is going to be a struggle for freedom with new energies, new possibilities unleashed, and the Lord's people better be ready to get on board. And I am talking about getting ready, because it is coming. Because there are those of us and yourselves out there who are dedicated to the proposition that it is going to happen.

But we are up against a lot and you had better have your own soul ready because you might be crushed like they tried to crush Fannie Lou Hamer. They tried to crush Dorothy Day. They tried to crush Michael Harrington. Tried to crush Abraham Joshua Heschel—a whole host of others. But that is what it means to talk about prophetic thought. You see, prophetic thought is something different than traditional academic discourse. Because it has to do with putting your life on the line but putting your life on the line, with the assurance that there is a faith that means you will do the right thing regardless of the consequence and you are not looking for a quick fix or a quick victory overnight.

T. S. Eliot says in the "Four Quartets," "Ours is in the trying, the rest is not our business." The question becomes, are we ready to try as we reflect on the future of prophetic and action? How do we deal with it then, this intellectual crisis? The fact that the notion of basic social goods as being independent of a market mechanism means that we must have a public sphere. We must have a nation-state that has enough resources to do this. We talked about this last night. There is a stubborn incapacity to generate resources for the public sphere. There are only three ways that you can provide resources for the public sphere. You either adjust the budget from one part to another, from defense to social support programs. You tax, or you continue to borrow money you don't have. Those are the only ways—the only ways you can do it. And we know the constraints: the national debt, the S&L crisis.

Right now they say the S&L crisis is going to cost $500 billion—for speculation under the Reagan administration. Economists tell us that we could eliminate poverty with $69 billion. Now, eliminate poverty is just not in the interests of poor people. It means you might be able to walk the streets with ease. It means you might be able to produce a quality labor force. It means you might be able to cut back on the expansion of prisons. You might even be able to envision quality relations between black and white folk.

Poverty is not the only source of the crisis but it is certainly one. But it has to do with priorities of a nation, and the role of any prophetic thinker and prophetic figure is to attempt to speak truth to power with love and humility. And if you believe as I do that for the last few years those in high places have been fiddling while the empire burns, then you speak the truth loudly and clearly and lucidly and you try to speak in such a way that it energizes and galvanizes folk who wouldn't ordinarily believe in themselves enough to do something. Because that is what it is going to take.

When we move now into our case study of black America, it has been the case that black America has served as a kind of moral conscience for the nation. Not because black people have a monopoly on virtue and the side of justice at all. Black people are as human as any other people in the world. But keep that in mind, because as most of you know, the very notion that black people are human beings is a revolutionary notion for the modern West. It cuts against the grain that was always there. Black folk are just as human as anybody else, ups and downs, strengths and weaknesses, ignorance and insights. But they have historically served as a moral conscience. I think Anita Hill is just the most recent in a long history of black folk raising fundamental moral issues and forcing the nation to come to terms with itself in light of its collective self-understanding and self-definition.

And so black America is both a thermometer as well as a projector of possibility for prophetic thought and action, given the historical situating of black folk. As most of you know, black folk in America don't even have a claim to being the most devastated people, even though black folk have known every humiliation and degradation and denigration. But that claim belongs to American Indians whose cultures and civilizations have been shattered by conquest. Killed off by disease and then roped into reservations and made citizens in their own land in 1924. It was an absurdity in many ways.

So blacks ought not to be making any claims about having a monopoly on oppression, but it is the historical situating of black folk in the United States, the crucial role of being enslaved people as 21 percent of the population. The crucial role of seeing America not as the great city on a hill, the last hope for human kind, but as an Egypt.

Josephine Baker in the 1920s wrote in her memoirs that "the very idea of America makes me shake. It makes me tremble and it gives me nightmares." I don't know of too many other people who could say that about America, because America is the land of opportunity. People from all around the world have looked to America for opportunity. Marcus Garvey was leading 3 million black people out of America in the 1920s. That is how deep the perception was of America's Egypt—cutting against the grain. Forcing America to see itself in a very different light. Not trashing America, not castigating America. Forcing America to see itself in a light which was not self-serving. Attempting to make it a better place by appealing to its own ideals. That is what I mean by a more conscious America. And the future of prophetic thought has much to do with the future of black America. And this a very important point that I think we have to grapple with, that it is impossible in the United States to think that the plight of black America is distinct from the plight of the nation.

When you drive through parts of northeast Tulsa it says as much about America as does driving through the suburbs. And that as an American citizen it has as much to do about you as it does me. It is not just a black problem. Not just a poor people's problem. Not just a social pathological problem. It is a symptom of a culture. It is a symptom of a civilization. And we've got to realize this. Because we are all on the same boat. It's got a leak in it. The winds are blowing and the storm is raging. We either hang together or we hang separately. And that is very difficult for Americans to come to terms with because the plight of black people has always been something you could hold at arm's length.

Look at the history of the debate in Congress over the Lynching Bill, introduced in 1903 and finally passed in the 1940s. This is something one can hold at arms length. No, the plight of these people has much to do with the possibility of prophetic thought and action. And what do we see among these people these days. We see an escalation—political consciousness. We see a hunger and a thirst for credible leadership—leadership of integrity. We see an unsettledness and an unease in black America. The first manifestations taking the form of Afrocentricity and narrow forms of black nationalism speaking to the erosion of self-love in the black community owing to the impact of market forces that have shattered the institutions that transmit self-love to black children. And we see a recognition of civilizations that predated the Age of Europe, that glorified certain individuals and accomplishments, that predated Europe.

I mentioned last night I believe that these are the first steps. They are in no way the last steps. Many of them are predicated on immature conceptions of self love as I noted.

Imitating the worst of Europe, putting down others at the expense of elevating ones self. But it is a form of resistance nevertheless. And this is especially so among those I highlighted last night—young people. Young people in black America are the vanguard of the quest for self-love and self-regard and self-respect. Hip hop artists, rap musicians. These aren't just young people trying to make money. They are young people who are responding to a shattered community, constrained opportunities, and are falling back on one of the two major traditions forged by black folk in the fire of oppression—the musical tradition. The musical tradition that has helped black folk stay sane. Singing through the storm. It has helped sustain the black person's sense of self.

The second tradition is the black church, especially the sermonic tradition, the rhetorical tradition. Of course hip hop in many ways is the bringing together of the linguistic virtuosity of the preacher and the African polyrhythms of earlier recordings, so that for the first time a whole new form comes together that expresses a deep sense of black rage and at the same time attempts to build on a distinct tradition created and conceived and constituted by black folk. It is the first stage on the way to something great. On the way to something bolder. And it is a tradition that has seized the imagination of young people of every color, not just in this country, but around the world. You could call it the Afro-Americanization of youth. And it is deep. It is very deep. It affects the way they walk. It affects the way they talk. It affects the way they view themselves. Isn't translatable fully into politics, but it shows the African-American stamp on the socializing of young people of any age.

We were joking here the other day about M. C. Hammer. Just a few years ago, he was a bat boy for the Oakland A's and he made $33 million last year singing and dancing. He is a business man. He's got his own production unit. He is not like the great Joe Louis, God rest his soul. Great American hero. Ends up having to serve in a position which was not commensurate with realities and his talent. Young black America says never again. The problem is that the black rage is boiling over and yet there is no channel to direct it. And that same black rage is catching on to other forms of rage. Look at Guns and Roses—it is all about white rage. Catching on—but no channel yet. Which makes it dangerous—makes it frightening. You need that energy. You need that rage but it has to be channeled.

I think it is no accident that Malcolm X now comes back not solely as icon but as the great hero for black young people. Of course you all know the hoopla over Spike Lee's new movie. He says it is going to be the greatest film in the history of cinema. I am not holding my breath, but God bless him. But the bruhaha over the Malcolm X film is that Malcolm X was in fact the major articulator of black rage in the last 40 years. And he comes back as an icon. But what's different on the one hand about Malcolm X, and Elijah Muhammed, Fannie Lou Hamer, or Martin Luther King, Jr., on the other was that he never was able to come up with an organization on his own that could direct the rage. It was only when he was with Elijah that the rage was directed. When he broke from Elija the rage overflowed. There was no direction to it and the conservative forces in American society were just waiting to express their contempt for black people, shooting them down like dogs. In Detroit in '67 or Newark in '67—or the 34 who died in Watts on August 11 1965. Which means that with the escalating political consciousness in black America, the boiling over of black rage from communities has little organization. I lecture in prisons all the time to some of the most articulate, intelligent folk in the black community. They have a lot of talent and a lot of time to read and reflect. Waiting to come out in order to make a contribution but there are no organizations. This leads us to the second dimension of the crisis. It's not simply an intellectual crisis, but an organizational crisis.

Without organization, that black rage will remain chaotic. That black rage will remain ineffective. My hypothesis is that when that black rage is directed with incredible organizations, with leaders of integrity, it will become contagious in other spheres in society because one of the observations that one can make about American history is that when black people advance, everyone else who has been suffering advances. Civil rights movement—struggling during Reconstruction—had links to the populist movement. Black people coming to the cities in the '20s and '30s, galvanizing new kinds of radicalisms. This galvanizing will also be the case, I suggest, in the latter part of this century. But to raise the question of organization is to raise the question of leadership, and if there is one common truism across black America, it is deep disappointment in black leadership. Profound disappointment in black leadership. We have to raise the question of why this is so. And there are a number of answers to this.

Today, you must be part of a process of compromise which does not allow you to speak with boldness and defiance about the realities that people are facing. To be a mayor—even a governor, a state legislator, that's fine, but you are on a different track. You can be progressive on the inside but your prophetic juices are not going to flow too easily. Of course black folk have rarely had folk on the inside. But when they get on the inside they discover they are like any other politician. They are concerned about the next election. They are concerned about their patronage system. And they are concerned about sustaining their constituency. Why should we expect different? Politicians are politicians, right? They might have a progressive tilt more so than some others. Maybe not. But when your leadership is in a strangle-hold by an electoral political system, that itself is constrained with an eroding tax base and eroding resources, it is no accident that prophetic thought and action, prophetic spokespersons become scarce. And in the meantime, various individuals emerge trying to fill the vacuum.

That's in part what's happened with Minister

Farrakhan. He sees himself in a prophetic tradition. He certainly speaks with a boldness and defiance against the white power structure, including black politicians, and he can draw 30 thousand people in New York City. And yet after he spoke for 3 hours, about 50 joined his organization. Despite what the press says—you know, the *New York Post* has it that "25 thousand black folk join Farrakhan's organization." You find only about 50 joined. But they came to listen to somebody who was going to speak boldly and defiantly.

In fact, the media will project Farrakhan as attracting black folk because he is anti-Semitic and black folk want to hear anti-Semitic rhetoric. There is no doubt in my mind that Farrakhan has deep xenophobic elements in his rhetoric, but that is not why the majority of black people come to listen to him, you see. They come to listen to him because he symbolizes boldness. And they don't join his organization because they don't see the kind of moral integrity that they want. And the press would have the nerve to tar the black community with the brush of anti-Semitism across the board and we know anti-Semitism is as American as apple pie in every sector of American life. Catholics, Protestants, right across the board. Yes, there is black anti-Semitism but there is anti-Semitism in every community.

Al Sharpton in New York City. You all know about Al Sharpton since I guess he has gone national now. God bless his soul. He is another example trying to fill the vacuum. He is in business as long as there is police brutality dehumanizing black folk. Which means he is going to be busy for a long time, unfortunately. Most of you know he was stabbed just a few months ago, trying to fill the vacuum. But no critique of the maldistribution of wealth. No critique of patriarchy. No critique of homophobia. Preoccupied with white racism. Significant but still too narrow and in many ways not prepared to the degree to which the black prophetic tradition of resistance and critique demands. I actually believe Sharpton is quite a courageous person in his own way—even given his narrow vision. Yet he is growing, maturing, expanding.

One can go on and on in this regard. But the question of leadership is fundamental because there can be no significant social motion, social movement without visionary and analytical leadership by people of courage and integrity. And it will not be one person. All messianic conceptions of leadership for prophetic action must be cast aside. We are talking about a collective form of leadership mediated by humility among those leaders in the collective. This is something new. This is something new. Jesse Jackson himself, given his own grand achievements, his brilliance, and his courage, still is part of that old messianic tradition. There is just one Negro out there. Head Negro in charge. No self-criticism. No accountability to the organization. Come in town, gone in 10 minutes, no infrastructure and institution left to keep things going. That's gone too. Takes courage to do it. I admire Jesse Jackson in his own way but he is part of a tradition that has to be called into question. We are talking about trying to get black action going again.

And of course, most significantly, there is going to be a lot of black women who are part of that collective leadership. The issue of including women is not a moral luxury. It is a necessity. You can't have an oppressed community that depends on 48 percent of its talent and think you can make it. You need all 100 percent of the talent. We see in black America talented, courageous black women. Look back to Ida B. Wells Barnett, Anna Cooper, Fannie Lou Hamer, and Ella Baker. But not just those. Women look back at their grandmothers. They look back at their aunts and their sisters and they see courage. That is why I respect Emma Mae more than I do Clarence Thomas. Because she is a struggler, invisible struggler. Not concerned about the limelight, but taking care of business. And you can't have a movement unless you have some TCB, some Taking Care of Business people, who aren't concerned about the limelight, who are all on the ground, laying the groundwork for the next wave of social action and social motion. And women would be both behind the limelight and in the limelight in this regard.

What, then, are going to be some of the strategies for the future for prophetic thought and action? Well, one will be that there must be a principle of coalition and alliance. What was distinctive about the 1950s when Rosa Parks refused to get up off the bus in Montgomery, Alabama was that it was a moment in American history in which the American left progressive forces had been wiped off the map by McCarthyism. They had deported 5 thousand. They had sent 4 thousand to Leavenworth—to jail, including the city councilman from Harlem named Benjamin Davis. A young preacher would take his place by the name of Adam Clayton Powell, Jr. And the Harlemites re-elected Ben Davis in jail. But he was in jail because of the Smith Act. Bold and defiant black folk. In the tradition of those who resisted in Tulsa in 1921 when a white mob attacked the black community here. Same tradition—resistance and critique.

A principled coalition and alliance. An all-inclusive moral vision that is willing to fuse with those women who will not put up with the degradation of patriarchy. Those trade unionists who are trying to expand the level of wages and benefits and control of work-place for workers. Those ecologists who are concerned about corporate abuse of land and air and those people of good will who proceed on moral principles, willing to join movements when they see credibility.

Part of the problem of American prophetic persons is that they feel as if there is nothing going on and so they keep their prophetic ideas to themselves. They are looking for something to do. They are looking for some bandwagon to get on if they think they can make a difference. But if they don't think they can make a difference, they sit back and say oh my God, I wish there were some actions going on that were open to me. And this has been part of the problem with black leadership. Progressive white folk have felt they had nowhere to go and nothing to do you see. So they remain complacent in the middle classes and stable working classes. Why? Because of a racially-polarized society. You've got some progressive white folk who wonder whether we're should even talk to black folk because they don't know whether they're in a bad mood or not. But they want to talk to black folks. So what do they do? Turn on Oprah. Turn on Arsenio or the Bill Cosby Show. There have to be possibilities and opportunities to express the solidarities of those progressive and prophetic white persons who are fundamentally concerned about the pervasive death and disease and destruction in America, especially in the black community. And there is not enough—there's not enough.

We were watching the baseball game last night. We got there late. My team lost. But one of the remarks that we made was, you see those black and white folk hugging each other, that is not superficial. It is real and it is real because they are in a context of struggle and bonds of trust have been forged. And they achieved something together, and America hasn't experienced that in the political sphere since the civil rights movement, with genuine, human interaction among black and white folk in struggle where bonds of trust are displayed. There are a lot of white folk who are hungry for that. A significant number who are hungry for that, who haven't found the occasion or the organization to express prophetic thought and action in America. A coalition has to provide that opportunity. Has to provide that possibility because there will be no significant change of the situation of poor people and especially poor people of color without trans-racial and inter-racial coalition and alliance. But it has got to be principled.

And you can wish that the need for coalition wasn't the case, but you must deal with the facts of the USA. black folk cannot do it alone. Black folk must fall back on their own resources as much as possible, but black America does not have the resources to deal with the deep problems of the black poor. There are two sources of resources in America, big business and government. Big business is not interested. It will be interested only to the degree to which it can be convinced that a quality labor force will result that can produce products of profitability. That is what it means to be in big business.

The government can do it if its priorities are right. Not programs of dependence that reinforce a passivity. We've got to critique certain aspects of the welfare state, yes. But we are talking about programs that give a lift to those who simply want a chance. And that same lift was given to Americans—disproportionately white Americans—after World War II. The creation of the American middle class was based on government programs. I mentioned them before: Federal Housing Administration; GI Bill; Worker's Compensation; Unemployment Compensation; Social Security. A majority of the American people support these programs, even under a Reagan and Bush administration. What they don't support are programs they perceive to be simply targeting a poor group of persons where they see no progress in their situation. And progressive thought and prophetic action must speak to universal programs that talk about poor people across the board even though it will disproportionately benefit people of color. Poor women—it will disproportionately benefit women of color—black and Brown especially.

What I am saying, then, in conclusion is that in reflecting on the future of prophetic thought it is inseparable from practice. It is inseparable in our individual lives of attempting to be exemplary to the degree to which we do live lives of love and struggle. The black church always used to say if the kingdom of God is within you, then everywhere you go you ought leave a little heaven behind. There is a deep insight there. Every blow you make is a blow for the kingdom, is a blow for freedom, is a blow for the expansion of democracy. The prophetic thought must be one that is broad enough to embrace all who are willing, whosoever will get on the freedom train of struggle. But at the same time prophetic thought recognizes that in the end, whether the social movement emerges or not, the struggle was worth it because we all still stand in the arms of God and that just the very privilege of being in this struggle is worth it. To serve and to give and to be inspired by ordinary creatures made by God who undergo suffering but who have the courage to project a different future and a willingness to fight for it, and you fight with them. That is the bottom line. Prophetic thought and prophetic action as I understand it. Thank you so very much for being so patient.

Questions

The questions were inaudible. Only the answers are available.

Question.

West: One of the things about racism is that, in my own mind, no one has fully accounted for it. It is a very complex phenomenon. It has to do with, certainly, economics. It has to do with controlling the economic opportunities of black people so that whites can move quickly further up the social ladder.

It certainly has something to do with sexual desires, because as we know racism is inseparable from certain sexual perceptions and certain perceptions of black bodies. And so notions of purity and impurity are very important. I recall I was 11 years old, I never learned how to swim, but I was asked to get in a swimming pool by my track coach. And I jumped in the pool and these white folk just started running away as if something was happening. I didn't know what was going on. But I had impurified the pool, you see. So the question became, where this notion of purity comes from. You see what I am saying? That is not solely economics. It has to do with a certain conception of human bodies and impurity. In this case black bodies are an impurity and that is one of the reasons why interracial sex is often at the center of the white mind in terms of interracial interaction. Because it has those notions of purity and impurity. But we never fully account for it.

And so there's these different levels of racism that we have to be able to talk about and acknowledge that we are all struggling with. None of us are in any way free of spot and wrinkle and yet we struggle as earthly vessels in this struggle against racism. And this is the kind of thing I think that needs to be reflected on and talked about so we can create bonds of trust. With no perfectionistic standards. This is very important. You can't go into the dialogue finger-pointing. "I am just going to wait for a racist's word. As soon as I hear it I am going to point that thing out right away. I've got you." See what I am saying. There has to be some context in which people come in, able both to be themselves but with a bedrock conviction that I am going to be struggling against racism till the day I die.

Question.

West: I think one thing to keep in mind is that black youth have always played a fundamental role in the black freedom struggle. A fundamental role—King was 26 years old. He lived only 13 years longer. Malcolm was 26. Those three students that sat down in Woolworth's in Greensboro in 1918—there was a student movement at Fiske University in the '20s—right across the board, young people have played a very important role. That is one of the reasons why I highlight what's going on among young people. Black Panther party in Oakland, October 1966, a 21-year-old named Huey Newton. Part of the reason is because older black folk have seen so many efforts come to nought and they are trying just to survive you see. But young folks still have a sense of spring. We call it spring consciousness—a possibility—a sacrifice. But what young people need, as you can imagine, is to read their history closely. To prepare themselves spiritually for struggle. To be self-critical and to be open to counsel from old freedom fighters who have been out there a long time. There is always a generational gap but it has to be lessened if the movement is to be as

The Future of Pragmatic Thought

effective as it possibly can. I think black young folk especially, but I think young people in general will play a fundamental role.

You look at the anti-apartheid movement on campuses six years ago—178 campuses those students were organizing across race, across gender for the sanctions. To insure that sanctions were in place such that business would not go on as usual in such an authoritarian state as South Africa. So the young people are very, very important. Very important indeed. In America in general and black America in particular. But the important thing is that they have to have a sense of history—what I was talking about last night. And when I began talking about 1955 when the Left had been wiped out, the young people who emerged were in a kind of historical vacuum because the links to earlier movements had been severed.

The National Negro Labor Council was a very radical group between 1949 and '53. The FBI had crushed them. Rushed into their offices. Dragged out the leaders, including Coleman Young who is now mayor of Detroit. He has become much more moderate over the years. He was head of that organization. They threw him in front of the House Committee on Un-American Activities and so forth. So there was a radical disjunction in '55. And in the '90s I don't think there will be that kind of disjunction. There is a deeper sense of history. There are a number of freedom fighters who are still out there in the nooks and crannies in our communities. In the universities there is now much more an openness to the history of struggle than there was in 1955. You think of what universities looked like in 1955. They were lily-white male affairs—for the most part well-to-do males. Even working class Catholics had difficulty gaining access, especially to elite institutions. That is no longer the case in the '90s. It was a different sense and therefore there are, in fact, new possibilities for support.

Question.

West: The question was what do I think of David

Duke, does it give me chilling effects? Well the first thing is we have to look at this as a symptom. What David Duke does is speak to the very deep white anxieties about downward mobility, using a rhetoric of scapegoating to provide some blame for why they are sliding down. And I must say that the crucial sectors of the white ethnic working class—their anxieties must be spoken to by prophetic figures. One must not write them off or there will be more David Dukes.

Question.

West: We will certainly pay a price for the David Dukes of this world but we pay less if we are better organized. One can steal the thunder from a David Duke if you are able to convince enough white ethnic working males especially that they cannot possibly get what they want out of a racist demagogue. Because what they want is an increase in their standard of living and an increase in the quality of life. This is what they want. And this is a perennial problem in American history and American politics. The strategy of making them feel as if their standard of living and quality of life will increase by blaming these black folk was used by George Wallace in 1968. Nixon used it to some extent in '72. Reagan certainly used in 1980 and Bush in the last moment, with Willie Horton, had used it. So a David Duke has to be looked at symptomatically.

Now on the other side, what David Duke does is wreak havoc with Bush because Bush has been using similar strategies. Duke is more explicit about it so it calls attention to Bush's strategies and Bush is on the run. Duke stands up on television and said I am only doing precisely what you do.

There can be no fundamental social change in the United States without creating cleavages and conflict among the power elite. Because they are not monolithic either. And to the degree to which they are in conflict and unable to reach consensus is the degree to which new possibilities loom for those below. They do consolidate, as they did after 1978, Business Round Tables, Chamber of Commerce, National Association of Manufacturers can all come together and say we are for deregulation. We are for givebacks at the negotiation table between workers and management. We are for slowdowns on social programs. We are for cutbacks of programs. We are for the build-up of the military budget. That was a consensus. And who bore the social costs? Most American workers. Especially non-supervisory American workers. They bore the social costs. They had the lack of increase in real wages and inflation-adjusted wages. Actually declined—that is the kind of message that needs to be put forth if prophetic figures are going to speak to the white ethnic working class.

And I'll give you an example, just very quickly. Take a look at policemen. Now who are policemen for the most part? Working people—disproportionately white but more and more black working people, you see. And they have to live every day dealing with the most immediate effects of the crises in America. But policemen have to deal every day with these kinds of crisis and they have low status. A policeman walks into a dinner party and says I am a policeman. People don't get down and say, interesting, like a professor. Interesting fellow. They say, a policeman—Oh my God. He's got low status or she has low status, constraint on his or her salary because the city is running out of money. But every day they get up, got to deal with crime, the drug situation, robberies and so forth. And of course you can imagine they feel nobody really talks about their situation other than when you do something wrong. Now that's true. Some of them are doing something wrong. But how do you speak to their situation such that one could bring them in? If it is possible; this is a challenge.

Same is true for teachers. Low status—low salary—they are teaching in those schools every day to the kids with broken families, hypertension, not enough to eat, empty stomachs, roofs leaking, outdated textbooks. Teachers and policemen—let them deal with the crisis. But their plight just tends to just get pushed aside.

Question.

West: Your question had to do with the separate school for black males and was wondering about the degree to which that was prophetic or not, and whether in fact that was a fulfillment of a certain prophecy that itself was based on certain segregationist principles and so on.

First, I think we have to recognize that there is de facto racial segregation in most of our urban centers already, based on residential patterns. We can give an account for why the residential patterns are what they are, that it has much to do with redlining of banks. We saw the recent study that the black middle class person is not getting a loan at the same level of white lower class worker—preventing a black propertied working class. Can't have a house without a loan in American society. So, redlining is very much a part of the de facto segregation in public education. For the most part you have schools that are already black. In certain places that is not the case, but most places that is the case. Then you have the shattered families and neighborhoods that I was talking about last night, so that education has always been a situation in which it is not simply what happens in the school room and school house, but also what happens at home and in the neighborhood. And they must work together for effective education to take place. Certain enforcements from parents. Certain reward systems put forward for kids who would want to do well and a sense of possibility in kids' minds in terms of education being a means towards something higher, you see.

Once that breaks down, then you simply have more and more de facto segregated schools based on residential patterning in which school becomes simply a place to be for a while but not serious investment in that place. The attempt to put forward policies of separate black male schools is a response to the desperate situation, as you can imagine. A response to the fact that education is simply not taking place the way it ought. Whether in fact separate black male schools is the answer to this is a separate issue.

I think there are some real faults of separate black male schools. Much of it has to do with the issue of the stress of black males at the expense of black females, reinforcing polarization within the black community. It is true that a higher percentage of black males are either in prison or linked to the prison system of some sort. One out or 4 now they say. But the crisis in the black community affects black males and black females alike. And has to be talked about in relation to one another. So that the stress on separate black male schools could in fact contribute to a prevailing patriarchal orientation that is in place in the black community. Some say the black man must indeed progress first before black women. And we saw that debate in the 1870s when they debated over who should vote, black men or women. Let the black men vote, we will get ours next year. They waited for almost 40 years. We have to come up with a way of talking about black communal interests that doesn't further polarize black men against black women, and I see the call for separate black male schools as reinforcing that polarization. But I can understand the motivation behind it even though I don't accept the reasoning. I don't accept the argument.

Of course, we are talking about the failure of public education. And when I talked about public education itself, being one of those basic social goods which would hold for children across the board. That has to be the higher goal even as the present very desperate situation continues to reign.

Question.

West: There is a sense in which the black community is an endangered species. I don't want to—as I said before I don't want to talk about black men independent of black women. We have a very different state but they go hand in hand. And so we are talking about a black community as a whole, and with black men dying early, murdered, going to prison, it weakens the black community as a whole.

Part II
Contributions to Prophetic Pragmatism

Part II
Contributions to Prophetic Pragmatism

The Postmodern Crisis
of Black Intellectuals

I would like to dedicate my brief presentation to the memory of one of the towering artists and great cultural workers of our time. I'm talking about none other than Sarah Vaughan, who was buried just yesterday in Newark, New Jersey. In fact I debated whether I would come yesterday or whether I should go to the Mt. Zion Baptist Church that helped produce one of the most subtle and nuanced voices of intelligence, insight, and pleasure-giving ever produced by this country and working within, of course, the great art form produced by working-class people in this century, namely, jazz.

I want to reflect briefly on the postmodern crisis of the black intellectual. And I must say that I actually did write a paper, but I decided it became relatively obsolete after this afternoon. So I thought that I would just attempt to speak directly.

The postmodern crisis: what do I mean by the "postmodern crisis" and what does it have to do with intellectuals of African descent at this particular historical and cultural moment? Well, actually I think it has to do with the fact that we are struggling with the vocation of political intellectuals, or what it means to be a political intellectual at the moment. Is it any longer a credible notion? And this is a very important question for me because, though I could be self-deceived, I understand myself to be first and foremost an intellectual freedom fighter. So the academy is only one terrain among many others.

So it might be the case that the very idea of being a political intellectual is antiquated and outdated; and that's the challenge. That's why the discourse about cultural studies for me is not first and foremost a question of area or discipline, but rather I understand it as the initial slogan used by a group of political intellectuals in Britain at a particular time attempting to bring to bear their own analytical tools, their moral and political vision and their sense of sacrifice, of giving their energy and time in order to fundamentally change Britain. And so Raymond Williams, Stuart Hall, and the host of others become not only sources of inspiration or simply models to imitate or emulate; no, what they become are exemplars of how they could keep the notion of being a political intellectual on the left alive in a world of shrinking options and alternatives for leftists. And that's in part what we're dealing with today, it seems to me.

And so when I talk about the postmodern crisis it has to do with the issue of the vocation of being a political intellectual. It's reflected on the one hand, of course, on the right, by Alan Bloom; and on the not-so-left by Russell Jacoby. I think that's one of the reasons Foucault and Said are so attractive to so many of us. It's not just the acuity of their analyses. I think Homi Bhabha is right; I think Foucault is indispensable, but his Eurocentrism and his Francocentrism stare at you on every page. That's called parochialism; no matter how sophisticated and subtle and nuanced it is, it's still parochialism, especially in the light of the call for Atlanticism, internationalism, and hybridity that Paul Gilroy and a whole host of others have talked about. But what Foucault and Said do speak to directly is the possibility of doing intellectual work in a world full of so much social misery and loss of social hope that we can justify ourselves as being significant in contributing to struggle. Because none of us can actually justify our pursuit of the life of the mind on sheer hedonistic grounds—because we like it, because it gives pleasure. It goes hand in hand with the hedonism promoted by the culture of consumption of a postmodern culture of advanced capitalist society anyway. There's nothing wrong with acknowledging that there's a hedonistic dimension to pursuing the life of the mind. But that's not all there is; there's got to be some moral and political grounds to this vocation. Thus the issue of vocation becomes very important indeed.

Why the term "postmodern"? The term postmodern becomes useful—though in many ways it does obscure and obfuscate—precisely because it helps us situate a new kind of culture being created in the midst of the restructuring of the capitalist international order. In that sense, Jameson is right. You may disagree with his laundry lists, he may misread particular cultural phenomena, but he's right in terms of understanding postmodernism not just as a set of styles and forms but as a cultural dominant of a restructured international capitalist order with its automation, robotization, computerization, its de-skilling of the working class, its re-skilling of the working class, and creating space for people like us: an expanding professional managerial stratum. We must situate the academy within this context of the postmodern crisis, given this restructuring of capitalism as we understand it. This is one of the reasons why I forever defend the insights, just as I criticize the blindnesses, of what was once called the classical sociological tradition, of Marx, Weber, Simmel, Lukács, Du Bois, and others. Blinding, why? Because there's very little talk about race, gender, very little talk about sexual orientation and anti-homophobic theoretical formulations, not just anti-homophobic moral gestures. But they're crucial because, when Simmel talks about objectification in the philosophy of money in 1900, he's talking about the degree to which there is an eclipse not simply of subjectivity but an eclipse of agency in which people no longer feel they can make a difference, so they view themselves as objects in the world. This is a very important cultural phenomenon; it's the first attempt, not even on the left as I understand it but on the left liberal side of the ideological spectrum, to provide a phenomenological description of the lived experience in capitalist society. This is, in part, what cultural studies ought to be about. Where are our phenomenologies of lived experience in advanced capitalist society? Jean-Christophe Agnew's book *Worlds*

Apart, which some of you may have read, is an attempt to do that, as a mode of historical reconstruction. Simmel's legacy is one crucial element of cultural studies.

The second key element is provided by Weber, of course, and he must not be downplayed. In some sense Foucault is a rich footnote to Weber. The extension of disciplinary order is in fact a certain twist of the extension of the iron cage, but at the level of micro-institutional practices. Why is Weber important? Because bureaucratization remains central in our lives. The ideologies of professionalism, of managerial perspectives, are part and parcel of the expansion of those institutions whose impersonal rules and regulations constitute deferential identities and subjectivities for us; that's what bureaucracy is about. All you need to do is to look at your University to see that. I just read a report in the *Chronicle of Higher Education*, that cites a 46 percent increase in the ranks of non-teaching professionals in our universities; that's a phenomenon Weber helps us recognize. But the larger point is that the analytical tools that are now necessary are part and parcel of this tradition, though it is a tradition that has its blindnesses. Just as we need Weber, we need Marx; among other things his concept of commodification is indispensable. I'm just finishing a text now on the continuing and considerable relevance of Marxist theory after Eastern Europe. Marxism remains important in part because it theorized commodification, and the process of commodification, especially in the form of big capital, especially in the form of oligopolies and monopolies, remains fundamental if we are to have any clue about how to talk about culture.

Herbert Schiller just wrote a book called *Culture Incorporated: The Corporate Takeover of Public Expression*. It's a kind of economistic Marxism, but a dose of vulgar Marxism is often necessary to keep us sober and "on the ground" in these days of cultural textualism. I don't advise stopping there, but he's got useful figures on corporate control within the most crucial forms of public expression, from the 32,248 "public" malls, which are not public in any serious sense—despite being among the few spots of public space left in late capitalist society—private property where the right to hand out political leaflets is denied, to his study of the American Library Association—the transformation of knowledge into a salable commodity as opposed to a social good; and why in New York City at this very moment libraries are only open four days a week. And they talk about black kids and brown kids not wanting to read. What are the objective conditions as well as the subjective conditions that folk used to talk about twenty, thirty years ago? Commodification. That is not, of course, a kind of catechistic retelling of Marx; it's an attempt to update where capital is and what's it doing and to what degree it is a source of so much social misery in the world.

These three processes for me become useful in trying to talk about the postmodern crisis because it has something to do with the fact that large numbers of people in the world, especially in American society, don't believe that they make a difference. Especially in the black community; that's what the meaninglessness and the hopelessness and the state of siege that is raging is in part about: the collapsing of structures of meaning, and the collapsing of structures of feeling such that hopelessness becomes the conclusion and walking nihilism becomes the enactment of it. How do you preserve agency? How do they think agency can be preserved given the resources available to them? And by resources I don't mean only financial and economic ones, I also mean cultural and existential ones as well—self-worth, self-regard, self-esteem, self-affirmation. Fundamental issues, if there's going to be any politics at all. And hence we see the decline in popular mobilization and the decline of political participation and the decomposition more and more of the institutions of old civil society, especially of old black civil society in the context of our shattered families and neighborhoods, and voluntary associations, with the market-driven mass media as the only means in which a person becomes socialized. I think, in fact, one way of reading rap music is as an attempt by certain highly talented cultural artists to socialize a generation in the light of the shattered institutions of black civil society; the families no longer do it, the schools can't do it. "How do I relate to other people? Tell me." And so they listen to Salt-N-Pepa who provide some moral guidelines as to how to relate to other people. They used to get it in Sunday school thirty years ago.

What does this have to do with black intellectuals? Much to do. Why? Because so much of American intellectual life, of course, now has been monopolized by the academy. I think this is a very, very sad affair but there's no way out. So that academicist forms of expression regarding intellectual work have become hegemonic. There is no doubt that one does indeed have to learn the language and learn the jargon in order to gain some sort of legitimacy, so that one can be heard by the main- and male-stream. There's no way around it unless we are able to sustain subcultures on the margins, but it's very difficult to do so because there are very few economic resources to sustain them. Unfortunately, almost every major intellectual today has to have something to do with the academy out of default, unless of course you're Gore Vidal who can go off to live in Italy off his money—God bless him! It's the only way to survive, though more and more move into journalism and mass media, becoming intellectual cultural workers outside the academy, but nonetheless forever feeding off the academy. And hence the kind of intra-class struggles that go on between journalists and academicians, struggles that I think are likely to escalate.

But there are other important points to note in talking about the academy. We know it's not only a place where there's tremendous competition for status and prestige, but that humanistic intellectuals are actually losing this competition. We know we're being marginalized *vis-à-vis* the technical intelligentsia. More and more we feel that what we have to offer has very little to do with the crucial role that science and technology play in advanced capitalist society. Even our legitimating role is being cut back, so many feel as if they can let humanist intellectuals do what they want to do as long as they speak only to each other; it seems they have very little linkage anyway to anything that actually makes a difference, other than the sustaining of their own careers. This is not my view; it's just a cynical view from the vantage point of a highly placed bureaucrat. Yet we also know that the academy has remained a major means by which working-class people have experienced upward social mobility. In that sense it's very different from the history of British University education, very different indeed. And in fact, I think for some of us the academy is a subculture of escape—and I'm not using escapism in a pejorative sense—but as an escape from the rampant anti-intellectualism in this country, the fear of critical sensibilities, democratic sensibilities, that is deeply ensconced within the parochialism and provincialism of the very people who we often invoke. And we recognize that the academy is a crucial terrain for struggle. This distinction between the academy and the world, of course, must be called into question. There are many crucial fields of forces and operations of power, and they criss-cross every institution in this society. There's no escape.

If you think you can go from the academy to the labor movement, to the church, or to some activist movement and not have similar fields of forces and operations of power at work, you simply have an academicist understanding of the academy. There's no escape. But that doesn't mean that the academy's a privileged site either. Not at all. The kind of work we've heard in the last day and a half ought to have taught us it is no privileged site whatsoever. But it also behooves us to think about the degree to which the waning of public spheres in this society tends to displace politics into the few spheres where there is in fact some public discussion—spheres like the academy. Hence so much of academic politics is a displacement of the relative absence of serious politics within the larger "public" spheres where serious resources are being produced, distributed, and consumed. And so much of academic politics—in terms of the level of what's at stake—seems to be exorbitant in a country in which our actual politics are comical. No real public sphere: we know about the theatricalization of our politics and the packaged character of our candidates and so forth.

Those political energies become rechannelled in the academic context in our attempt to talk about pedagogy. I think this is a lesson that we can learn from John Dewey. Dewey actually became preoccupied with pedagogy after he moved to Chicago in 1894. He moved the year of the Pullman Strike, and he concluded (it's one of the reasons he was silent on the Pullman Strike) that labor could never win in America in a direct confrontation; thus he had to engage in his own kind of politics, cultural politics. A cultural politics that would highlight the role of education in providing new perspectives, critical alternative orientations to lead toward what he thought for awhile would be a serious confrontation of capital and labor. John Dewey was a Democratic Socialist for sixty-five years. He concluded that the political left based on class struggle could never win, so cultural politics became his major terrain for contestation out of pessimism about the American Left. This deep pessimism about the American Left ever winning, even imagining the American Left winning, deeply affected John Dewey's politics. We can take some clues from this, not from the pessimism, but from the struggle with it. Hence the crucial role of pedagogy, but we also need to keep open the notion that pedagogy can never be all there is, that there must be some grass-roots organization and mobilization if there's ever going to be serious left politics in America.

Let me say a word about the role of cultural studies in the postmodern crisis as it relates to black intellectuals, especially like myself. Because it seems to me that what we need first is to read very closely the kind of narratives and tales that have been told about cultural studies by Stuart Hall and others within the British context. The traveling of cultural studies to the United States must be met with a critical reception—and by critical what I mean is an appropriation of the best: acknowledging where the blindnesses were, while discussing to what degree British cultural studies can be related to the U.S. context.

We did not do that with deconstruction and you have seen the results. It's true: the promiscuous formalism in which every text can be turned against itself in order to show the degree to which every ground can be undermined, including the very ground that is put forward to undermine it, and so on and so forth. There's still power there, though I won't go into the positive moments in deconstruction, since I'm highlighting the degree to which there was an uncritical reception. This is also true for Michel Foucault. Foucault cannot be understood without understanding his early years in the Communist Party, his polemics against the French Left, the degree to which a Marxist culture was so deeply influential on the Left Bank, and Foucault's own attempts to create new left space in relation to those various tendencies and elements. That's what a critical reception of Foucault, or anybody from anywhere, is about. We can learn much, to be sure, but not without knowing our own intellectual history or without considering how the U.S. context will receive these texts. This is the question. Who, for example, reads Thorstein Veblen's *Theory of the Leisure Class* in talking about cultural studies in the United States? Go back and take a look at Paul Sweezy's essay on Thorstein Veblen in the 1952 *Socialism and American Life* volume that Princeton University put out. Why did Paul Sweezy, the leading Marxist intellectual at the time, think Veblen was a crucial figure in terms of our cultural realities and in the light of his Marxist theory? I'm not saying he's right, but look at the dialogue—there is a tradition of very important left cultural reflection that can provide a site upon which intellectual cross-pollination with the best of Williams and Hall and Rowbotham and others can take place in the US context. We could say the same about Du Bois; we could say the same about Charlotte Gilman Perkins; we could say the same about F.O. Matthiessen. One can work one's way through U.S. intellectual history by tracking the contributions of progressive thinkers.

Now part of the problem is going to be the degree to which American studies—given its own history as told by Kermit Vanderbilt in his recent text *American Literature and the Academy*, or Richard Ruland's earlier book on the recovery of American literature—either welcomes or resists this interchange. The history of American studies is in some ways parallel with cultural studies in Britain. But the major objects of attack in the U.S. were not left Leavisite perspectives, or even Eliot's elitism, but rather New Criticism and its different ideological trajectory. Yet we also should examine certain American Marxisms: the Marxism of Granville Hicks, of V.F. Calverton, and other American Marxists attempting to create their own left American cultural studies in the thirties and the forties. Of course I'm being quite fragmentary, but I'm trying to give you a sense of how we can tease out a dialogue between the British and U.S. traditions within the U.S. context. It's not a matter of Americanism in the life of the mind. America indeed has something to contribute without our succumbing to atavistic patriotism in intellectual matters. We're talking about trying to keep our eye on analytical tools that have, in fact, been put forward and in some ways sharpened by intellectuals on the American terrain who should have been in contact with what was going on in the late fifties and sixties and seventies in Britain. But we must not commit the same mistake by looking to see what's new, while forgetting about this American tradition. This is precisely how theory actually leads one astray in ways that Stuart was talking about.

Stuart mentioned today the degree to which there was, in fact, a Marxist moment in cultural studies in Britain, and then critical breakthroughs with feminism and race. I think Douglas Crimp was correct to say we need to highlight the homophobic moment as well. But in the United States it is very, very different. As Richard Slotkin, Michael Rogin, and others have stressed, the U.S. begins with the dispossession of Native American lands. And the continuing racial encounter is there from the very beginning, with Mexican peoples and African peoples. America starts in part with the expansion of European empire and these racial encounters. The country commits civil suicide over the issue in the 1860s. By describing this as a starting point, I don't necessarily mean to privilege it exclusively; I simply mean it has a lot of weight and gravity in any story that you tell. How can the reception of cultural studies in the United States not put race—not at the center (we're not making claims for center and margins)—but give it a tremendous weight and gravity if we're going to understand the internal dynamics of U.S. culture? There's no escape. It's a different history than the formation of the British Empire with its attempt to relegate race to the periphery and resist its intrusions within the metropole. Yes, race is there in Britain, as we all know, but with very different histories, different developments. And similarly so in terms of gender. And, of course, when we look at the academic interventions what do we see? In '69 there was a movement for Afro-American studies. It was not a Marxist moment because there were very few Marxists around in '67-'68 in black America. Ten years earlier most had been thrown in jail and deported, so there's discontinuity in terms of the Marxist trajectory in this country. They are radical, oppositional, some are subversive. How do we understand the moment of the intervention of Afro-American studies in the Academy? Let's read that history next to the intervention of cultural studies in Britain.

Women's studies offers a comparable picture. Where are all the Marxist women's studies people in 1968-69? There aren't too many, certainly not a tradition that's developed. But they went back and recovered a radical tradition, a long rich tradition of feminist thought and praxis in the United States. Let's read the intervention of that particular construction and creation over against the construction and creation of cultural studies in Britain and talk about how interfertilization at this moment can create deeper insight and enable more effective praxis.

I want to say a word about how this relates to popular culture, because we know what happens—especially after 1945 in this country—is by means of the classic Fordist formula of mass consumption creating mass production. We can recall the creation not only of the first mass culture but the creation of a mass middle class, or at least a mass working class with a bourgeois identity that understood itself as middle class. So popular culture, mass culture, becomes fundamental for the creation of American culture after 1945. And postmodernism and its attempts to undermine the division between high and low culture has much to do with the fact that it's a profoundly American phenomenon, one dealing with the pervasiveness of popular culture (given U.S. economic hegemony) in Latin America and in Europe with the Marshall Plan. And so that popular culture, Hollywood, music, film, radio, becomes fundamental. If you're going to understand what is going on in American culture, given this distinctive development that is different than any other capitalist nation at that time, given its world hegemonic status, you must come to terms with popular culture. Of course there's also the matter of understanding the degree to which you've been shaped by it. When I talk about Sarah Vaughan—and I could talk about Baby Face or Marvin Gaye or a host of others—I'm talking about people who help keep me alive. I'm not just talking about some ornamental or decorative cultural object of investigation! These are people who make a difference in your life. James Brown makes a difference in my life, that's a fact. That doesn't mean he's the only one, but the point is that when we talk about popular culture we're talking about its materiality at the level of producing and sustaining human bodies. Or at least at times convincing that body not to end its vitality and vibrancy, not to kill oneself. That's in part what culture does; it convinces you not to kill yourself, at least for a while. Which means that, of course, it's breaking down in parts of American society, as suicide rates suggest. But I'm getting way off the track. The important point is that popular culture mediated by mass commodification becomes crucial in the U.S. context. It's very different in other places around the world.

And this leads me, of course, to religion. We could trot out facts: 97 percent of Americans believe in God, 75 percent believe Jesus Christ is the Son of God, and we say, "Oh, God have mercy, I've struggled up here and we've got all of these fundamentalists out here." Why is that so? What is it about religion as a cultural phenomenon in this distinctive capitalist nation that makes it so crucial? This is a crucial question, especially if you're an activist, because you'll be bumping up against all these folk who have all these strange beliefs, from your point of view. This is very important. This is something that the communists who were looking to Europe in the 1930s and 40s could never understand when they went into the black community. They would say, Paul Robeson, intelligent man that you are, your brother is a bishop in the A.M.E. Church, you're the son of a preacher, and you still have such a respect for the black church, but you're too intelligent for that. "Kiss my so and so, I'm the product of a rich tradition," Paul would say. I'm trying to use a concrete example to give you a sense of the degree to which we have got to attempt to understand what goes on in a complex phenomenon in this country: Namely, all of the various religious sects and groups and cults and denominations and temples and synagogues and all the other religiousforms of association through which folk come together. How do we understand them, especially as potential for broad progressive and oppositional praxis? These are fundamental questions. It's very different in Britain, where the working class rejected religion a long time ago.

What does this have to do with black intellectuals? A great deal. Why? Because I still follow Gramsci's injunction to know more and preserve the links in broader civil society. Stuart said it with insight today: by knowing more it means you've got to be rooted within subcultures and subgroupings and traditions, intellectual and political, and yet also be conversant with the best of what's going on about the academy—which means you sleep less, because you have to know more. But you know more not in order simply to know more, though it is a lot of fun, but you know more in order to make your links better. So when you're rooted in the broader institutions in civil society, whatever they are and in whatever role—the trade unions, the mass media as a cultural worker, or in musical production or video production, or a preacher, or what have you—you have the roots required for what you have to say to bring some insight, and yet your insight can be informed by the very folk who you're talking to, because they have a wisdom to bring. And it provides the context for struggle, so that bonds of trust can be generated that will sustain you when the police come after you, as courageous Michael McGee may discover in a few weeks in Milwaukee, God bless him. I like his spirit of resistance no matter what you think about his tactics. There's too much death going on, he says, somebody else got to die too. There's something about that moral ground. I have trouble with this, but I also resonate with his sense of desperation because I've also seen too much death, too much despair. That's the kind of spirit of resistance you need, but that's the challenge of a kind of linkage that must be forged in order to rechannel that kind of energy into a more effective and efficacious progressive project.

That's what the aim is; that's what the project is all about. And that's going to be the challenge for black intellectuals in particular, as well as for progressive intellectuals in general. I hope that we can overcome the virtual *de facto* segregation in the life of the mind in this country, for we have yet actually to create contexts in which black intellectuals, brown intellectuals, red intellectuals, white intellectuals, feminist intellectuals, genuinely struggle with each other. There are very few contexts for that. Prince's band is more interracial than most of the intellectual dialogue that goes on in America. That's a requisite, that's a precondition for the emergence of the kind of thing that Jackson and others have envisioned, namely a Rainbow politics, which is the only means by which fundamental social change is going to come about. It may not be Jesse who leads the coalition, but we know it's got to be some multiracial coalition, an alliance, and that might not be strong enough in and of itself; it might all get crushed. Capital's powerful but we must take a chance, take a risk. But there has to be some intellectual coming together, not closing of ranks but coming together, before there can in fact be possibilities for this kind of flowering and flourishing. Not because intellectuals will lead, but rather because there must indeed be a role for theory if we are to understand the circumstances against which we're struggling and if there are going to be visionaries who have the courage to lead it. And there will be leaders. They may not come from us, probably not, but come from a host of various sources. But they must have tools available, and we can contribute to that. Hence, there is a role, there is a function, there is a possible vocation for cultural studies in the academy, no matter how overwhelming the odds.

Discussion: Paul Gilroy, bell hooks, Cornel West

Question (unidentified): I want to ask about commodification. In the past when we used the word, we were saying that there's something bad about it. It seems now that there's some uncertainty about that. I wonder whether you think that in the current period we have to give in to this idea that markets are necessary—or can we rehabilitate the vision that markets could be done away with?

Cornel West: That's a very complicated question because commodification, as initially used by Marx in the "Fetishism of Commodities" chapter had to do with the transformations of relations of human beings into relations of things. For Marx it had to do with a certain relation of domination, of workers selling their labor power, their energy and time and so forth, to employers. The market was the primary force for objectifying people. Simmel argued that was not just the market; there are a whole host of other forces that were doing this kind of objectification. By the time you get to Lukács you have something different, in many ways more profound, partly because he read Simmel and Weber. In that crucial chapter in *History and Class Consciousness*, which I still think is necessary reading for any serious left cultural thinker, he has a very new understanding of commodification as a cultural phenomenon, linked to market forces, that has to do with how subjects are constituted. You are asking about how one goes about arranging economies in light of present day alternatives. Command economies had commodification and objectification under Stalin. Were there markets? Of course there were markets. The problem was who regulated them—the bureaucratic class. We could go on and tell a long story. So when we talk about markets these days, especially given all the kinds of fetishizing and idolizing that are going on in the markets these days, we've got to raise the question of what are the conditions under which market operations take place. Do I believe that markets are inescapable for the economy? Yes I do. The best explanation of this, I think, is Alex Nove's book *The Economics of Feasible Socialism*. Why? Because democratic ideals can in fact be promoted only if we can sustain levels of productivity. But that's a different kind of discussion, that's a discussion about how you arrange economic affairs. And about sustained levels of productivity so that you don't have a lack of commodities in a society which falsely claims that they don't have commodification, which is one of the results of the low productivity of the command economies, and so on. I think it's important that one unpack and tease these various levels out in talking about it.

Paul Gilroy: I hear in your question an echo of a deeper question about Marxism itself and about what I would want to call the productivism of Marxism and about whether or not Marxism can survive the productivism being extracted. And for me here the issue is really a question of growth, and how we can move towards a political vision which, in asserting this link between sustainability and justice, actually says that the overdeveloped countries must give up that growth.

Question: You seem reluctant to talk about deconstructive thinking. Why are you not willing to say how can we appropriate this in the same way we're trying to appropriate British cultural studies, Marx, Weber, etc.?

West: In another essay (published in *Out There: Marginalization and Contemporary Cultures*) I argue that there's something quite positive about deconstruction, having to do with keeping track of the rhetorical operations of power and binary oppositions. And this can provide new openings, and it has been quite powerful in relations to race, gender, sexual orientation, and so forth. The problem is that it too easily becomes linked to an austere epistemic skepticism. And that austere epistemic skepticism makes it very difficult to make the links between rhetorical powers, military powers, political powers, social powers, and other kinds of powers. I see this also in Foucault. Foucault doesn't tell us anything about the nation-state, he doesn't tell us anything about nation-states bumping up against each other. But you can't tell a history of the modern world without telling a history of nation-states bumping up against each other, like August

1914. These are serious silences about macro-structural operations, about which Foucault has very little to say, and Derrida has hardly anything to say. So when it comes to issues of the materiality of linguistic practices, Derrida and Foucault are very important. This is what Stuart Hall described in his paper. Marx doesn't talk about the materiality of language at the level of perspicacity and acuity that Derrida and Foucault do. Marx throws it out in *The German Ideology*, but it's flat, it's wooden, he doesn't follow up on it. So that there is a crucial set of insights that come from deconstruction. But what I'm really fighting, as you can imagine, is the American reception. That's what makes my blood boil. And the reason it actually boils is this: I said that one crucial element of the restructuring of this society in which we live is the expansion of the professional managerial class or stratum, and we're part of it. That means that we're getting a lot of resources that other people are not getting. And some of them are your cousins and my cousins, they're working-class people. They're poor people. Collapsing educational systems, and we get these lectureships and fellowships that are proliferating all the time. I'm in Italy this month, next month I'm in New Brunswick and then California. Where's all the money that *we* get coming from? How come that money is not going to some of the failing educational systems, in Chicago and New York and Houston? I'm not trying to be ugly here; what I'm saying is that we're part of the restructuring, we're part of the new class. And we have to be self-critical; this is what critical self-inventory is all about in a Gramscian sense. So the question is how do we fight as progressives and co-opted? And at the same time how do we understand the degree to which the larger structural institutional forces that help enable some of our activities might actually be siphoning off a whole host of resources from other people who need it badly? And that's a much larger discussion about educational policy on various levels of elementary school, secondary school, community colleges, state colleges, and in elite institutions. But we have to be aware of those kinds of discussions and dialogues, it seems to me. It's not that what I'm saying is necessarily true, but we need to talk about this in a serious kind of way.

bell hooks: I want to ask how, in the U.S., cultural studies can avoid simply reproducing a more sophisticated group of people who are interpreting the experience of the "other" under the guise of identifying themselves as comrades and allies.

West: As the humanities as a whole is being marginalized, *vis-à-vis* the technical intelligentsia, cultural studies becomes one of the rubrics used to justify what I think is a highly salutary development, namely interdisciplinary studies in colleges and universities. But it differs from one place to another. Here in Champaign-Urbana you have persons who were exposed to cultural studies when I think it was at its height in terms of vitality and vibrancy. I'm not saying that things are dead now, but I think that the Birmingham school in many ways provided such an exciting context in which issues of vocations, of being political intellectuals, of struggles over the Marxist traditions, struggles over the feminist challenge, struggles over race were going on. The legacy is still alive but it was at its heights, I think, and people like Larry Grossberg at this particular place were part of that. So that they're able to bring that experience to bear upon their own institutional context and remain in contact with Stuart Hall and others in Britain as they have continued to work, have made this place very different than a lot of other places who just are starting their cultural studies projects right now. At different institutions, they're going to have to deal with levels of professionalization and specialization that are very different than what has been established here at the Unit for Criticism and Interpretive Theory. Look at CUNY, there's tremendous advantage where you've got Stanley Aronowitz and a host of others who are also in contact with and producing some of the best critical theory being done at the time. That's going to be very different than some other places. So one would have to make assessments in light of each and every place.

Gilroy: I want to caution Cornel against that enthusiasm for some inevitably reified memory of what was going on at Birmingham. I mean I feel a bit the way Miles Davis feels about the definition of musical authenticity in which he got trapped, when he said he was there and actually it wasn't like that.

West: I like to think that it was, though.

Gilroy Well, maybe as an imaginary, it's OK.

West: Sure. But you'd say that about my religion too, wouldn't you?

Gilroy: Yes, I would. The point is that the answer to bell's question depends not on anything which is intrinsic to cultural studies, but on factors which are external to it. There are no guarantees in any heuristic idea of cultural studies. If people can struggle to rescue something from it which enables them to face three ways at once and to hold on to some notion of themselves as interventionist scholars, then great. But if cultural studies becomes a fetter on that, then I imagine cultural studies will have to be left in the distance. And I think that's what Stuart called the moment of danger, but it's likely to be longer than a moment.

Question: I'm struck by the fact that there are more people of African descent from London here than there are from the United States. I'm wondering if the importation of the Birmingham model and its representatives, however useful, might inadvertently silence both an indigenous African-American tradition and living, practicing African-American activist scholars in the United States today?

hooks: I think that Paul Gilroy touched on that in his paper by saying that part of our oppositionality as peoples of African descent, globally, has to involve countering that impulse by being just as engaged in the work of Paul Gilroy, Stuart Hall, etc., as other groups of people. I think that's just beginning to happen in African-American intellectual thought right now. where do we look to for our references, as African-American intellectuals? Who are we reading? Who are we teaching our students to read? I don't think, in a white supremacist context, we can't counter the fact that people might want to play off black British intellectuals against black intellectuals in the U.S. I think our best opposition to that is the kind of collective solidarity that comes through global awareness of our connections.

Gilroy: Yes, I agree with that. I think there's a lot more work that has to be done in making those links something vital. When you look at the nineteenth century material, it's impossible not to be struck by the fact that they were closer to each other than we are. Considering the space-time distanciation of the world, that's an extraordinary thing to appreciate.

West: Let me just say a quick word about the silencing of Afro-American intellectuals in this country. I think that there is an intellectual and social chasm between large numbers of persons in Afro-American Studies programs and persons in interdisciplinary studies, or cultural studies. Now why does this chasm exist, that's a much longer story that has to do with what particular schools of thinking have shaped significant numbers of Afro-American scholars who are in Afro-American studies programs *vis-à-vis* the kinds of developments that have been going on in literary criticism and cultural studies and so forth. There is this *de facto* segregation, when we actually look at what some of the dynamics have been in a variety of different institutions, between black scholars and left intellectuals.

Gilroy: Isn't that a consequence of the fact that reification and institutionalization aren't only problems of cultural studies? I mean I almost feel like I want to shift it slightly back the other way and say that these are issues which are intrinsic to the nature of the Academy. Cultural studies doesn't have a monopoly on that difficulty.

West: Yes, but you sound a bit too Marxist on this one now. It cuts deeper than that. It's not just a matter of reification and commodification, specialization and bureaucratization, and so forth. It has to do with the very deep racist legacy in which black persons, black intellectuals are guilty before being proven innocent, in terms of perceiving them capable of intellectual partnership, capable of being part of a serious conversation. I think that traverses the processes that Paul is talking about. And so it makes it very difficult indeed, and it's part of the larger struggle against the racist legacy in this country as it's manifested in this case.

hooks: We can think about this in terms of the construction of film criticism and the lack of black people doing film criticism. Look at how Spike Lee has been constructed in popular culture as if there were no other popular black filmmakers ever. Most of us continue, never seeing, never hearing of Oscar Micheaux, who made 38 films between 1918 and 1939. When we think about "the insurrection of subjugated knowledges," we have to think about where those subjugated knowledges are going to surface if the very construction of popular culture is such that it says to people that black filmmaking begins with Spike Lee. And so when I have black students who want to be filmmakers, I ask them if they've thought about how much we need people to write about film. How much we need to go back and talk about Oscar Micheaux's vision, as a person who saw himself as making films for black people that would deal with the complexity of their lives. We have more complex representations in Micheaux's films than in most films we can see right now by black filmmakers, particularly in terms of his representations of black females, because he wasn't trying to reach a cross-over audience; there was no such thing as a cross-over audience.

Itty Abraham: I would like you to comment on a kind of black nationalist rhetoric in which it seems that the removal or reduction of oppression for African-Americans can only come at the cost of the oppression of other minorities.

West: The historical records show that the progress of people of African descent in this country tends to go hand-in-hand with the unleashing of new opportunities for large numbers of people far outside the black community, from women to peoples of color, to the handicapped, to the elderly, and so forth. I think you are talking about a certain kind of rhetoric of desperation that comes from certain black nationalist corners, given what they perceive to be a zero sum game. And therefore, when they see that progress is not being made, they assume that some other group is making it. And that is an expression of frustration, but it is far removed from the historical record. I think that distinction must be made and all of what I have said is not only an attempt to expand that historical record but to insure that the struggles of the people of African descent go hand-in-hand with struggles of people of color and working people and people of good will across the board. That doesn't mean that we're going to sidestep this struggle over the crumbs that often occurs among peoples of color; it doesn't mean that we're going to eliminate the resentment and envy and jealousy that some people might have for other peoples of color who seem to be moving rather quickly up the social ladder. That's a cultural phenomenon, it's there. At the normative level, of course, I find myself very much in agreement with what I perceive the historical record to be: black progressive movement going hand in hand with other progress. But this does not occur easily.

Question: This, too, is a question about the interrelationship of forms of oppression. You made reference to rap as a cultural resource providing moral guidance. What is the nature of that guidance and how we theorize it?

hooks: I think we have to talk about the production of rap, as well as about what rap is listened to by whom. Because in fact there are black men who are doing feminist raps, anti-rape raps. But we have to talk about the kind of African-American culture that is being produced for a cross-over audience. Take for example a production like *House Party*, which we know to be homophobic and misogynist. Now is this because "black culture" is homophobic and misogynist in some more intense form, or is it in fact that when racist white spectators go to the cinema one of the things that makes that cinema more enjoyable is if there are certain kinds of things that can be hooked into, including certain kinds of stereotypes about black people, i.e., that black people are more homophobic than other groups in this society. Black people are homophobic and xenophobic, but not necessarily more so than other groups of people in this society. We have to keep that in mind, too, when we talk about rap. Because it's a minority of rap people who are doing the sorts of things that are getting a lot of attention, including misogyny, homophobia, and anti-Semitism. And so we have to ask, why are people focusing so much on those forms of rap? Why do we not read about black men who are doing anti-rape rap? Because that's not as interesting!

West: I think it is very important to say that rap is not monolithic, homogeneous, that there are a whole host of different kinds of raps. I invoke Salt-N-Pepa just as an instance of a certain way of responding to black patriarchal practices and the black male predatory lust towards black women's bodies. And they have certain ways of black women's bodies responding to that. Moreover there are dominant forms among these various forms of rap, and they're highly problematic in terms of moral guidance. But it's not as if they could actually go to other sources and find significantly less patriarchal guidelines. If they go to church, they're going to find patriarchal guidelines;

if they go to some other institutions of black civil society, they're going to find it too. So it's not as if U.S. society is overflowing with sources of anti-patriarchal values and practices. But there are some sources there and some of these rap musicians are trying to provide them, but the ones who do it are not dominant.

Wan-Ling Wee: I wonder why discussions of race and class in Britain never discuss the Chinese in Britain?

Gilroy: I don't know the answer to that question. I think it's probably got to do with who owns and manages and controls the spaces in which such discussions appear and the particular definition of race politics that they want to trade in. I really don't know how to account for it beyond that. I think when we talk about the question of race in Britain, you have to appreciate that the numbers of people involved are actually tiny by comparison to the numbers of people involved in this society's minority ethnic groups. I don't see in the development of those particular political spaces any attempt to address the diversity and the differences which exist within those minority ethnic communities in our country. Also, these discussions are often involved with a very specific political project which has to do with a particularly economistic definition of Marxism and the attempt to advance that within a very familiar pattern of political organization. The reason that those other experiences aren't addressed or recorded as having any significance is because they're perceived to be peripheral to where the real action is supposedly identified. And it's hard to imagine where the forces that could shift that parochialism will emerge from. Presumably from within those communities themselves at some later stage. I don't mean to sound complacent about it, but I do want to say to you that those kinds of publishing are probably much more peripheral than you imagine to the lived reality of the experiences, not just of Chinese people, but of the very ethnic groups in whose name the kind of authority to speak is actually derived.

Constance Penley: I appreciated your exhortation that pedagogy is not enough. Of course it's not enough. But the way you couched that exhortation built upon a polemical separation between politics and what goes on in the university. You claim that an academic discourse in politics is just a displacement from wider politics, what goes on "out there." I've heard this stated several times throughout the conference; Henry Giroux always makes reference to the ivory tower, the academy; Janet Wolff said that it was crucial that cultural studies be off in its own isolated enclave; Jan Zita Grover said that she didn't know what went on in terms of activism within the university and implied that she didn't think much did. I think that a lot goes on there. Pedagogy goes on there. For most of us, that's our political practice. And we're doing more than just canon-bashing. When I look around at what's going on at universities around the country, I see people trying to get issues of sex, class, race, and anti-homophobia made into a public discourse. I see a new move to eliminate the military, and fraternities, and the CIA off campus. There's a lot of work that's being waged against the increasing corporatization of the universities. People are working all the time to increase the number of women and minorities among the students and the faculty. There are still divestment struggles going on all across America. I think we might want to look at our need to imagine that we are working in a place that is without politics.

West: I think you picked up a tension in my presentation, I won't call it a contradiction (I like Stuart Hall's term, though I get it from Paul Tillich). As you recall, I said that this distinction between the academy and the world had to be called into question because all we had were fields of forces and operations of power. If you take that line, you and I are on the same wavelength, because the same powers that work in the academy work elsewhere, and the struggles that you talk about are oppositional in the same way in other contexts. I would say over and over again that the academy's a crucial site. On the other hand, in my own attempt to move from context to context, we have to recognize that there's still a level of privilege in the academy that makes it very different from other sites in civil society. And that level of privilege cannot be overlooked even as we agree with what you say. The university is a crucial site but a different site. It has its own kinds of privileges that do promote, sometimes, an insularity, and a parochialism, in the name of being cosmopolitan. And it's this other side that might lead you to infer that somehow I might be part of this cast of voices that seems to be trashing the academy, which I do not want to do at all. But I'm not sure I want to lose the tension, either. I think I'm going to go to the grave with that tension.

Gilroy: Isn't the point about cultural studies that it helps you preserve the tension and work with the tension, which is not to say that the tension does not need tuning?

hooks: If this conference had been called "Feminist Cultural Criticism: Now and in the Future," a lot of people would be talking about the kind of political agency that is produced in and extends beyond our classrooms. There would not be this sense of separation between the classroom and some outside because what we so overwhelmingly see is the continuity between them as people come to critical consciousness in the feminist classroom. The dynamic and momentum of cultural studies that most excites me is that it has helped me to teach many marginalized groups the joy of theory and theory-making, and how it is linked to a political practice. Part of what keeps me in the academy is seeing it as a field of contestation; it is in the context of a liberatory feminist pedagogy that I see enormous kinds of change, the kinds of education for critical consciousness that moves out beyond the academy precisely because the issues of race and gender touch people in how they live in their everyday life. And I think that's part of the joy of the kind of work many of us are doing.

Arlene Torres: I am concerned about the use of the term "subculture." What does it mean, and what does it say about African-Americans, Chicanos, Puerto Ricans, Asian-Americans, and Native Americans, considering that most of us have been largely absent from this conference?

West: When I talk about subculture I mean primarily just me and my partners trying to keep alive a particular left project in my neighborhood. I mean the black intellectuals, let's say, in parts of New York City, who come together every other week to try to stay sane. I mean that little small subculture that helps keep you going, discussing the issues, doing what you do next in terms of your project. What that group that talks through you thinks about police brutality, what you think about what's going on in Milwaukee: that keeps that kind of dialogue going. It also provides deep emotional networks of support and so on. That's what I meant by using that term to talk about a crisis of black intellectuals. I'm not talking about a deeper methodological issue about the culture of Chicanos, or the culture of Chinese or Asians and so forth. I agree with you that at that deeper level one has to contest the use of such a term.

Donna Haraway: I grew up in a town in Colorado where I thought the Atlantic Ocean began somewhere in Kansas and that anything that happened East of Kansas City counted as the East Coast. And I know Cornel grew up in California, but I think maybe you've been in the East too long. Paul's Atlanticist reformulation of African heritage, African culture, and African-Americans, reformulated a lot of issues for me. But it's a California statement I want to make. It has to do with seeing the world in relationship to Latin America, Central America, Mexico, leaving in conquest territory so that it almost seems like Quebec is part of California rather than part of the world you're talking about. It's the sense of the Pacific. I think of Bernice Johnson Reagan's speech on coalition politics which took place at a West Coast women's music festival and is an absolutely canonical text in U.S. feminist circles and in the constructions of the category, "women of color," but also of a feminist cultural politics and a vision of a new world cultural politics. None of this is caught by the tendency to build the world as black/white and America/Britain, with a little bit of Australia and Canada thrown in. This particular global mapping leaves out these really crucial questions.

Gilroy: I didn't want to push the thing about the Atlantic too far for many of those reasons. I suppose for me what was important about trying to do that was that I feel that most of the decisive political battles are actually going to be registered at that intermediate level, between the local and the global. And I wanted to actually try and illustrate what it might mean to put some concepts in there in a very provisional way. And I hope it didn't sound as if the Atlantic was supposed to exhaust that; that was just an instance. I think we've got to try if we want to face the future instead of looking back over our shoulders. We've got to try and be a bit more imaginative about what those intermediate identities, concepts, localities, loyalties, are going to be. And I think we need a new topography and I think that maybe, I'm not even sure about it, the Atlantic thing might be part of that.

Question: I was particularly taken with Cornel West's engaging comments concerning the intellectual life of the mind. I have some concern about the *de facto* segregation of the life of the mind. I don't know if you have any kind of recipe for making the mind more culturally plural, but I certainly would feel a lot better leaving this conference if you would share such with us. When I start to think about the classroom which attempts to teach cultural studies with attention to race, as you so desire, I try to imagine who indeed will teach in that classroom, and how we can be sure that that person will not abrogate the responsibility to all of the constituents who come into that classroom. And furthermore I wonder to whom the constituency will address itself once it leaves the classroom, once it has graduated and goes out. Because I have great fear when I look around this room, and I really do wonder about the number of African-American men and women who will take their places to teach cultural studies. I think about the violence of one-year appointments and two-year appointments, and I hear this rumor that there is a lack of blacks with PhD.'s and I know of blacks with PhD.'s who don't have appointments at all. These kinds of things are disturbing when you are talking about the crisis of the black intellectual. I'm particularly wondering about why you chose not to address issues of safety, feeling safe as being a reason for not speaking, a reason for not teaching as the very basis for silence. I wondered that you did not address the very real problem of the fact that there is violence in the classroom. And when one does go through the very harrowing experience of attaining the credentials needed to enter the academy, one black person walks into the classroom, the white students break into tears and rush out. These are very real issues for those of us who sit on the other side of the desk. And I wonder, could you tell us something to help us to have hope?

West: I think what you've said is quite real. I was just touching the surface of this issue when I talked about gaining cultural resources. How do you build up a context in which self-confidence can be acquired? In which you are able to conceive of one's self, not only as being part of the conversation, but as being taken seriously? The idea of taking black people seriously in the life of the mind is a very new notion for white people, so they have to get used to it. Now, it's true that among white progressives it's a bit more distributed than among the larger white society, but they suffer from the disease too. So the question is how you create conditions that will facilitate taking black people seriously in the life of the mind. Which means giving them the benefit of being wrong; we can't be right all the time, or we're not being taken seriously. Which means they also have the benefit of being right, and you can be wrong, and so forth. Now, we could just call that human interaction, but the idea of human interaction across races is a new notion in Western Civilization at some levels, especially at the level of practice, as Gandhi noted quite aptly. So the question is, on this individual level, how do we insure the possibility of this kind of human interaction? I think one way of doing that is by creating very substantive links with colleagues who you are sure are in touch with your humanity and you are in touch with theirs, in affairs of the life of the mind. That's very important. I'm speaking personally now. When I think back on my own formation, what was it that sustained the intellectual part; I had a lot of the other parts on different axes, but the intellectual part had to do with being part of a network that was involved in that kind of critical exchange in which one's voice is a serious voice. That's very important. And one finds it among a small group usually—sometimes it might be just one or two—and one hopes that it's across racial lines, not always, but one hopes. At that very individual level, that's one way of sustaining hope. The problem is that many of our students don't experience that, and hence the life of the mind becomes something that's completely alien; it's a white thing, it has nothing to do with what I'm about, and they move in other directions. And of course, they still will pursue the life of the mind in their own way, but it will be linked to a very, very different kind of project, owing in part to not experiencing that kind of human interaction with teacher, with peer, with friend, with colleague, whatever it is. I think that's one way of doing it. More importantly it has to do with the larger picture: race relations in America. As they deteriorate it will be reflected and refracted in the universities and colleges and so forth. And even in California, Donna, Farrakhan will draw thirty-five thousand people, which is to say it's still part of a black/white discourse. You can talk about the multicolored, the multiracial, and so forth, but a certain black nationalist rhetoric that is still operating in a binary oppositional discourse is still quite powerful in Los Angeles and Oakland. So that those deep resonances are there, and the question becomes, how does one understand that kind of black nationalism as a way of affirming one's sense of self-worth? But then, how does one rechannel it in such a way that the multiracial and multicultural character of California in its actual population becomes reflected in one's left politics in the black community? And that's a struggle that we have all the time. I recognize that the issue of identity, positive identity, self-affirmation, and holding at bay self-doubt and self-contempt and self-hatred, is an indispensable element for people of African descent. This is the great lesson of Garvey. You can disagree with Garvey's politics but his cultural insights are profound. And that's one of the means by which students can feel empowered to take the life of the mind seriously in all of its various forms as they move towards the kind of progressive multiracial vision that Donna, myself, and others have talked about.

Decentring Europe

The Contemporary Crisis in Culture

I am very glad to be able to come to Pittsburgh, and give this memorial lecture for James Snead. I think it's very important that we recognize in the life and work of Brother Jamie that he represents a new breed of black intellectuals who were produced by those cultures on the underside of modernity. And by "new breed" what I mean is that, given his energy and the quality of his mind, he was willing no longer to confine himself to the Afro-American terrain, but rather to try to redefine the whole in the light of his understanding of that terrain. When we look at his work—be it on Joyce, be it on Mann, be it on Faulkner, be it in this powerful reading of "Benito Cereno" which remains unpublished (and I hope will be published one day) and a host of such essays, as well as his pictures—we see Jamie as, in many ways, a symbol of a new generation of black intellectuals, self-confident, no longer anxiety-ridden, no longer looking for the kind of approval and legitimacy in the eyes of their white peers, but willing to flex their intellectual muscles and move in whatever directions and trajectories that they choose. It is a very new movement, a very new movement of black intellectual life. This came out in recent conversations I had with St Clair Drake. Now St Clair Drake is of course one of the towering figures in American social science, a black intellectual who wrote the classic *Black Metropolis* in 1945. But in talking to Drake, I was telling him about James Snead, and was telling him about the work that Jamie and I were doing together and which will be completed: producing black analysis of Afro-American culture—from culinary black practices across black intellectual practices, and so forth. And St Clair Drake was saying to me, "You know, there's a sense in which I recognize myself in what you describe James Snead to be, and there's a sense in which I don't." There is a break, there's a discontinuity, a kind of disruption that has occurred. Now St Clair Drake is 78 years old, trained at the University of Chicago (1954, PhD). And when I go back and think about five wonderful years with James Snead, meeting him at Yale in 1984 and reading his works and having many, many conversations (the last being at MLA at New Orleans, just this past December, to complete our characterization of what we precisely wanted to do in our text), I think St Clair Drake is right. And I think the legacy of James Snead, the grand contribution of Brother Jamie, will be something with which I myself and Professor Henry Louis-Gates Jr., who is here in the audience, and a host of others will have to engage, and we will have to ensure that we hold up that blood-stained banner in a way that would make Jamie proud.

Let me begin to talk a bit about my subject, "Decentring Europe: The Contemporary Crisis in Culture." I think it's almost obligatory these days to begin with an historicist gesture to contextualize and pluralize, to trash the monolithic and the homogeneous in the name of heterogeneity and plurality and multiplicity, to acknowledge the degree to which we're concerned now with the concrete, the particular, with the hunger for the concrete and particular. Yet it seems that we still remain in a kind of rhetorical orbit, feeling as if we're on the ground but not really, not really. This historicist moment (interesting to see how long it will last), but this historicist moment means then, I want to suggest, that the dominant mood of theoretical activity goes back to demystification, something that itself had been trashed in the name of deconstruction and sophisticated austere and epistemic skepticisms. And by demystification I mean the notion of explanation now comes back beyond simple description, be it thick description, descriptive mappings and so forth. That explanation begins to come back in relation to the mobilization of meanings, and structures of domination—once more, sits on the agenda. The Marxisms, the feminisms, the various anti-racist, anti-homophobic forms of social theory begin to come back with power, and we're concerned with the degree to which operations of power are still hidden, are still concealed.

What I want to argue, in fact, is that when we talk about contemporary crisis in culture, the one way of beginning to come to terms with this is having to historicize and pluralize and contextualize the postmodernism debate. That's what I've come here to do in memory of James Snead. To historicize the postmodernism debate and try to come to terms with what precisely is at stake. How does it relate to the vocation of the intellectual, given the challenge of the technical intelligentsia, given the challenge of the middlebrow journalist? What kind of role and function can the humanistic intellectual have in advanced capitalist society, given his or her placement within the academic's life of the professional managerial class of this particular society?

For one begins this by going back, and that's precisely what I'd like to do. I want to provide a mapping of postmodernism by examining four major cultural critics of modernity: Matthew Arnold, T.S. Eliot, Lionel Trilling and Frantz Fanon. This mapping shall be guided by three fundamental historical coordinates: first is the legacy of the end of Europe, of what it means to live 44 years after the end of the age of Europe, when those nations between the Ural mountains and the Atlantic Ocean are no longer at the center of the historical stage, and what are the ramifications and repercussions of living in such a time, given our role as cultural critics, given our role as intellectuals. The second, of course, has to do with the ascendancy of the United States as an uncontested world power and issues of hybridity and heterogeneity in its concrete sense, namely in this new world nation, the first new nation that had to deal with hybridity and heterogeneity in a very, very real sense, given the dispossession of the land of indigenous peoples, and the story that we all know to be the constitution of what America—as an ideological construct and, of course, in its concrete embodiment—is all about. And the third historical coordinate is that of the decolonization of the Third World, the exercise of the agency and the new kind of subjectivities and identities put forward by those persons who had been degraded, devalued, hunted and harassed, exploited and oppressed by the European maritime empires. These three large historical coordinates are linked to the four critics—linked to Arnold, Eliot, Trilling and Frantz Fanon.

Now in the popular mind, postmodernism is usually understood as a set of styles and sensibilities and forms associated with either historical eclecticism or buildings, the return to the decorative and the ornamental reference of older styles, for example, works of Venturi and Charles Jencks and Robert Stern. Of course, we know, even the postmodern movement in architecture now is passé, very much like deconstruction is passé in literary criticism, and yet there are still residues. There's also an association with the confusing denarrativizing strategies in literature of Barthelme, Ishmael Reed, John Barth, Thomas Pynchon and others. And I think Thomas Pynchon is probably the towering figure in this regard. Just as crack is a postmodern drug because in the culture of consumption, we live in a culture which forces us to be addicted to stimulation at its highest level, and crack, of course, is the highest level of stimulation known to the human brain. Pynchon is dealing with the wasteland and the repercussions of the wasteland, and the ways in which advanced capitalist society has tried to recycle it through the consumption cycle in such a way that it generates addiction and stimulation. Yet Pynchon still holds on to critical intelligence to bring the kind of credibility to the debate, by fusing his understanding of Eliot's metaphor with the attempt to hold on to some sense of agency "that keep cool and care," which underlines, of course, his classic, *Gravity's Rainbow*, 1974.

Postmodernism is also usually associated with increasing incredulity toward metanarratives—the Lyotard definition. I happen to think Lyotard is excessively overrated. But when you actually look at "increasing incredulity towards master narratives" and see the religious revivals and the ideological revivals and the national revivals—be they in the Second World, Eastern Europe and the Soviet Union, or in the First World, or Khomeini—you say, whose? who is he talking about in terms of increasing incredulity toward master narratives. He and his friends hanging out on the left bank, whom does he have in mind? And then, of course, his readings of Kant and Wittgenstein are quite middlebrow. But of course these are cheap shots—I'd defend them if I had to—but these are cheap shots. But the important point is that in using Lyotard as a kind of launching pad, it shows just how narrow our academic inscription actually is as critics; just because he writes a book that the Canadian government in Quebec asked him to write, and as a Frenchman he titles it *The Postmodern Condition*, somehow it becomes an important text. Deleuze is a much more important figure, overlooked because he doesn't translate in part, but that's another story and has to do with where the travelling theories come from, why certain theories do come in the way in which they do, and the ones that stay home, or the versions of the ones that stay home. Deleuze, of course, came to us in *Anti Oedipus* as opposed to the author of Nietzsche and Hume and Spinoza. That's the more challenging Deleuze.

On the one hand, then, in the popular mind, postmodernism is associated with these particular impressionistic perceptions I am putting forth. On the other hand though, it is important to note the degree that postmodernism is an American phenomenon. And here I think Andreas Huyssen is right—in his "Mapping the Post Modern," that wonderful essay in *After the Great Divide*, in which he talks about postmodernism as being initiated, first among architects, and later painters, writers, photographers, and critics, who revolted against the domesticated modernisms of the museums, the academy, and the gallery network. The academic mind is right then to note the degree to which issues of difference, of marginality, of otherness, of alternity and subalternity, of being subjugated and subordinated do indeed become very important parts of the problematics of postmodernism that was raised in such a way that it appropriates late transgressive modernists—the French going back to the Nietzsches, Mallarmés and others.

And yet on the other hand, it is a profoundly American phenomenon. Why? Because in fact it is the response to the degree to which modernism became part of the ideological arsenal used in the cold war against the Soviets, and the attempt of younger artists, painters, architects, and others to revolt against the modernisms whose own transgressive power was seemingly highly circumscribed, diluted, absorbed, co-opted, and so on. So where does that leave us? Well, it leaves us, it seems to me, in a situation in which we have to acknowledge the degree to which the struggle over what we understand postmodernism to be and historicize it, raises issues of historical periodicity in the ways Jameson talked about, so insightfully, and also blindly, if we are to read Jameson dialectically, as he attempts to read others. But the issue of historical periodicity is very important. Why? Because then we begin to raise the question: Well, if we're talking about the postmodern moment, what do we understand by modernism, what do we understand by modernity? And it hints of course at the kinds of discourses that we have these days on what we understand a modern to be, noting the variation within the conception of the modern (modernism, modernization, postmodernity, and so forth), every conception of which is linked in some way to our understanding of when it began, when it peaked, when it declined, and whether it ended or not, and such a definition is linked to how we conceive of ourselves and how we conceive of the possibility of social change in the present moment.

Now I'll begin with the legacy of the age of Europe because postmodernism, I'm understanding, is a set of responses due to the decentring of Europe—of living in a world that no longer rests upon European hegemony and domination in the political and economic, military and cultural dimensions which began in 1492.

Given the slow but sure Europeanization of the world, as we know, the European nation, by 1835 owns, well, 35 percent of land and peoples on the globe, and, as Said has pointed out over and over again, by 1918 almost 85 percent of peoples and land on the globe. It is the reshaping of the globe within one's own image. Now it's not a monolithic image, but it is, broadly speaking, a European imposition willed upon the world in the colonial and imperial form. Two major cultural critics that highlight the modern crisis during the last decades of the age of Europe are Matthew Arnold and T.S. Eliot. The contribution of Arnold was that he acknowledged religion—the glue that fragilely held together the old aristocratic-led regimes in the sixteenth, seventeenth and eighteenth centuries could not do so in the nineteenth century. As did Alexis de Tocqueville, Arnold saw that the democratic temper was the wave of the future. He thereby proposed a new conception of humanistic culture that had to play an integrating, cementing role in the state and emerging secular bourgeois capitalist society. His famous castigation of the immobilizing materialism of the declining aristocracy, the vulgar philistinism of the emerging middle classes, and the latent explosiveness of the working majority was motivated by his desire to create new forms of legitimacy, authority, and order in a rapidly changing moment—late nineteenth century Europe. For Arnold, this new conception of culture "seeks to do away with classes," he says, "to make the best that has been thought and known in the world current everywhere; to make all men live in an atmosphere of sweetness and light" (taken from *Culture and Anarchy*).

This is the social idea—men of culture are the true apostles of equality. The great men of culture are those who have had a passion for diffusing, for making prevail, for carrying from one end of society to the other. Keep in mind the Gramscian notions of hegemonic activity as the saturating of a culture with a set of values and sensibilities, a set of ways of life and ways of struggle to reshape it in such a way that culture has institutional elaborations and apparatuses set in place. So to talk about power/knowledge in this regard is something very concrete, and Arnold, I think, understood it very well—but to make prevail from one end of society to the other, "the best knowledge, the best ideas of their time"; "to divest knowledge of all that was harsh, uncouth, difficult, abstract, professional, exclusive," this is still Arnold, "to humanise [culture], to make it efficient outside the clique of the cultivated and learned, yet still remaining the best knowledge and thought of the time, and a true source, therefore, of sweetness and light."

It was as an organic intellectual of the emergent middle class, as inspector of schools that led an expanding educational bureaucracy, as professor of poetry at Oxford, the first non-cleric and the first to lecture in English rather than Latin (Professor Jonathan Arac has talked about this in his powerful essay on Arnold in *Critical Genealogies*, his recent text) that Arnold defined and defended a new secular culture of critical discourse, lodged in the education of periodical apparatuses of modern society, that would contain and incorporate the frightening threats of an arrogant aristocracy and especially an anarchic "working majority." His ideal of disinterested, dispassionate, and objective inquiry that would regulate this new secular culture of critical discourse in its justification of using state power to put down any threats was widely accepted. I think one of the most telling sentences in Matthew Arnold's *Culture and Anarchy* is: "through culture lies not only perfection but our safety." And this notion of culture is something that provides a kind of fortress against threats, so that the safety or survival of this cultural critical discourse is something that becomes part and parcel of holding on to the best of the past. And this idea of safety maybe had something combative in mind. Maybe it was going to play a crucial role in terms of containing as well as incorporating those who were potential threats to this culture, and need we forget, of course, that powerful metaphor in the last section of *Culture and Anarchy*: those who are a threat to this survival, he said, why, you throw off your Tarpeian Rock. And of course he has appropriated that metaphor from his father, Thomas. The Tarpeian Rock was where late imperial Rome cast out convicted murderers. And as we shall see, the use of state power enables you to cast out not only individuals but whole cultures.

For Arnold the best of Europe was modelled on Periclean Athens, Elizabethan England, and late republican/early imperial Rome. It is important to remember that Arnold believed, like so many who lived in Europe in 1850, that Periclean Athens had no links to northern African civilization. Martin Bernal and a host of others have begun to contend this reading in which Greece, as an ideological construct, is separated from the African continent, hence is autonomous in some sense and has no link to the very people or their traditions which will be subjugated in the name of European civilization. But in Arnold's view, the best of the age of Europe would be promoted if there was an interlocking affiliation—the emerging middle classes, a homogenizing cultural critical discourse in the educational university networks, and the state (this is *the* connection—the state on the one hand, the set of institutions that has a monopoly on the instrumentalities of violence in the culture, that has a monopoly on its administration; at the same time the university, bureaucracy and the emergent middle classes). The candidates for participation in the legitimation of this grand endeavor of cultural renewal and revision would be the detached intellectuals willing to shed the parochialism and provincialism and their class identities. Arnold calls them aliens—persons who are mainly led not by their class spirit, but by a general humane culture, by the love of human perfection. Now needless to say, this Arnoldian perspective still informs many of our academic practices and cultural attitudes even given the passing to and fro of different schools of thought, and so on. Why? Because it is inscribed in the practices and the institutions of higher learning from the moment that Johns Hopkins breaks from ecclesiastical authority, in 1876. And Hopkins itself was modelled on the German universities of the nineteenth century, they themselves taking as a model the University of Berlin, the first great modern university. The Arnoldian institution is one that gives to persons like ourselves who are socialized in a cultural way—into this culture of critical discourse—some sense of who we are, a sense of identity, even displacing our early identities. It moves us beyond our early lives, sophisticates us, refines us, makes us part and parcel of the world of educated gentlemen and, later, gentlewomen. And this Arnoldian model is still operating in part. Our views about the canon, about admission procedures, about collective self-definitions as intellectuals, are still marked by this conception.

Yet Arnold's project was disrupted by the collapse of nineteenth-century Europe, which comes of course in August 1914—World War I; in George Steiner's words, the first of the bloody civil wars within Europe—the very definition of it as a "world war" shows how Europe misrepresented itself in relation to the globe—a civil war within Europe that brought to the surface, not the violence of the masses that Arnold feared after the Hyde Park riots had violated middle-class space and gardens, but rather this violence of the state, of the very institutions Arnold valued, the violence of the state itself. In the ashes of the vast human carnage of its innocent civilian European population, Thomas Stearns Eliot emerged as the grand cultural spokesman. He would say, "Have strength to force the moment to its crisis." His image of Europe as a wasteland of cultural fragments with no cementing center, a chamber of horrors, loomed large. And though his early poetic practices, I would want to argue, were much more radical, much more international than his critical practices—a point I think that needs to be made over and over again—it was very clear that Eliot posed a return, a revision of tradition, capital T, as the only way of regaining European order, authority, and stability. For Eliot, too, contemporary history becomes as James Joyce notes in *Ulysses*, a nightmare from which he is trying to awake, or as in Eliot's review of that masterpiece—in the *Dial* of 1923—the immense panorama of futility and anarchy. In his influential 1919 essay, "Tradition and the Individual Talent," Eliot writes: "if the only form of tradition of handing down consisted in following the ways of the immediate generation before us, in a blind or timid adherence to its excesses, 'tradition' should positively be discarded. We have seen many such simple currents soon lost in the sand, and novelty is better than repetition." Tradition is a matter, he says, of much wider significance. It cannot be inherited, and if you want it you must obtain it by great labor.

After his conversion in 1927, Eliot found his tradition in the Church of England, a tradition that permitted him to promote his Catholic cast of mind and his Calvinistic heritage. Like Arnold, Eliot was obsessed with the idea of civilization and the horror of barbarism, or more pointedly the notion of the decline and decay of European civilization. With the advent of World War II, Eliot's obsession became a reality, again. Unprecedented human carnage throughout Europe, as well as around the globe, put the last nails in the coffin of the age of Europe. After 1945 Europe consisted of a devastated and divided continent with humiliating dependence and deference to the USA, on the one hand, and of course after Yalta, to Joseph Stalin's USSR on the other.

The second historical coordinate, then, is the emergence of the USA as the world power (in the words of André Malraux, the first nation to do so without trying to do so) which sets the immediate context for the emergence of the problematic of postmodernism, of difference, of heterogeneity and so forth. The USA with, in the phrase of

Henry James, its hotel civilization, a unique fusion of the centrality of the market and the stress on the warmth and security of the home, precisely what a hotel is. Highly suspicious both of the common good and the public interest, highly privatistic, individualistic—in short, a country unprepared for world power status. I'm sure you're all acquainted with the way that F.O. Matthiessen, that great American critic, a left critic from the middle part of the century, said, "Is in fact the United States the first modern nation to move from a stage of perceived innocence to corruption without a mediating moment of maturity?"

It's not a cheap shot. He's trying to understand something about the nature of this first new nation that is thrown upon the scene, given the ashes of the end of the age of Europe. How would it undergo its maturation, what form would it take, and how would it deal with its own problem of heterogeneity and hybridity, especially given, of course, the legacy of slavery and the legacy of its patriarchy. Yet with the recovery of Stalin's Russia, which had more than 20 million dead compared to the 385 thousand dead in the States, the USA felt compelled to make its presence felt around the globe with the Marshall Plan to strengthen Europe against Russian influence and provide new markets for U.S. products. With the 1948 Russian takeover of Czechoslovakia, the 1948 Berlin blockade, the 1950 beginning of the Korean War, the 1951 establishment of NATO in Europe, it was clear there was no escape from world power obligation, from imperial obligations. It was clear that the thrust of the nation's history would force it to constitute itself as an empire, given the collapse of European maritime empires, as would the Soviet Union, slowly but surely, constitute itself as an empire. The post-World War II period in the USA, the first decades of what Henry Luce envisioned as the American century (it would only last 28 years, from 1945 to 1973), was not only one of incredible economic boom, but also cultural ferment. It was not simply the creation of a mass middle class, the first society in human history to make the shape of the social structure appear like a diamond, with the majority being in the middle, with the poor being a minority. But, also the emergence of the first major subcultures of American non-WASP intellectuals, as seen in the so-called New York intellectuals around *Partisan Review;* or seen in the abstract expressionists in painting of course, when the world of painting shifts from Paris to New York; or seen in the bebop jazz artists, the first black intellectuals being taken seriously as part and parcel of the new art form that was distinctive and novel in the new world (something that Dvorak understood way off in Czechoslovakia, and he looked at the new world to see what was new, and incorporated it in his "New World Symphony")— Charlie Parker and Dizzy Gillespie, and a host of others. This emergence signified a challenge to an American male WASP elite, loyal to an older and eroding European culture in which Arnold was the major model. The first significant salutary blow was dealt when assimilated Jewish-Americans entered the higher echelons of the academy and, slowly but surely, anti-Semitic barriers began to unravel under pressure of alliances with those liberal WASPs who were willing to at least entertain a few refined assimilated Jews within their WASPy terrain. Lionel Trilling is an emblematic figure in this regard. This Jewish entry to the anti-Semitic exclusivistic and patriarchal culture of critical discourse in the elitist institutions of higher learning initiated the slow but sure undoing of male WASP cultural hegemony as well as homogeneity. The contribution of Trilling was to appropriate Matthew Arnold for his own political and cultural purposes in his doctoral dissertation. Professor Daniel O'Hara's recent text, *Lionel Trilling: The Work of Liberation,* the best treatment that we have of Trilling up to this very moment, is a reading of the degree to which Trilling is trying to reshape a new kind of consensus, a liberal, anti-communist consensus for the new emerging middle classes in the new empire, in the new American empire—using the values that we associate with Trilling, of course—complexity, difficulty, modulation, and so forth and so on. Again, those values and features that became the badge of the intellectual climate, holding off what was perceived to be the Manichean discourse of the Left, and at the same time the philistinism of mass culture in television, emerging film, radio, and so on. The same kind of Scylla and Charybdis orientation going on—mass culture, on the one hand, and left politics on the other.

The postwar boom laid the basis for intense professionalization and specialization expanding institutions of higher learning, especially in the natural sciences, partly in response to Russia's successful venture into space. This forced humanistic scholars to search for new methods in order to buttress self-images and to be rigorous and scientific and serious, and so forth. New Criticism became, in fact, a useful way of appropriating highly serious and rigorous methods that had to do with not only close readings of texts, but also buttressing self-images of these humanistic intellectuals. But it was, of course, a New Criticism that was severed from its ideological roots. This is also true, I think, in other disciplines—be it the logical precision of reason in analytic philosophy, the jargon of Parsonian structural functionalism in sociology—all providing languages into which persons could be socialized and could be viewed as having scientific self-images, vis-à-vis their scientific peers, which is to say vis-à-vis their peers in the natural sciences. Yet towering cultural critics like C. Wright Mills, Richard Hofstadter, and W.E.B. Du Bois bucked the tide. And I think it's interesting that we don't have any serious treatments of these figures.

Trilling, in his famous essay on the teaching of modern literature, asks the question, "Can we not say then that when modern literature is brought to the classroom, the subject being taught is betrayed by the pedagogy on the subject?" It's true. "We have to ask ourselves whether in our day too much does not come within the purview of the academy. More and more of the universities liberalize themselves and turn their beneficent and imperialistic gaze upon what is called life itself. The feeling grows among our educated classes that little can be experienced unless it is validated by some established intellectual discipline," which is Trilling's point. You can mention the fact that university instruction often quiets and domesticates radical and subversive works of art, and that it then turns its objects into merely habitual regard—this process of what he called the socialization of the antisocial, or the acculturation of the anticultural, or the legitimation of the subversive, leads Trilling, and I quote, "to question whether in our culture the study of literature is any longer a suitable means for developing and refining the intelligence." This is the same Trilling, of course, who had gone to Columbia in the 1920s and had been taught the famous slogan of John Erskine, "You have a moral obligation to be intelligent." How, in fact, do you sustain, cultivate and refine critical intelligence? And Trilling is reaching a point where maybe in fact the teaching of literature is just another big Baconian idol that gets in the way of the cultivation of intelligence. The question becomes, what is the alternative to this for Trilling? He asks this question not in the spirit of denigrating or devaluing the academy, but rather in the spirit of highlighting the possible mobility of an Arnoldian conception of culture to contain the overwhelming philistine and what he perceived to be the anarchic alternative. It was these alternatives that were becoming more and more available to the students—on the one hand mass culture, and on the other hand radical politics. And it is this which leaves Trilling world-weary at the end of his life. He felt that, in fact, the space that he had tried to create—that liberal space—was collapsing and there was no possibility of holding back the anarchic forces on the one hand—the radical students—and on the other hand, the mass culture. And we know now from some of the notebooks that Trilling did enjoy television, especially Kojak. But that's another matter.

This threat is associated with the third historical coordinate that I'll end with, namely the decolonization of the Third World. It is only when we take this process into account that we can grasp the significance of, on the one hand, the end of the age of Europe, and, on the other hand, the emergence of the USA as the world power. The first defeat of a Western nation by a non-Western nation—Japan's victory over Russia in 1905—the revolutions in Persia in 1905 and Turkey in 1907, Mexico in 1911, the Soviet Union as we know in 1917, on up to the major break in 1947 with India, Ghana in 1957, Guinea, and so forth and so on. This shaping of a very different world, a very different world indeed, in which the way in which decolonization takes place serves as a source of radical interrogation of the Arnoldian model of culture as well as that appropriated by Trilling, let alone, of course, a return to the tradition put forward by Eliot. The first thing to note here is the centrality of violence, the degree to which a person begins to recognize just how ugly and brutal the world really is. Not simply, of course, the mushroom clouds of Hiroshima and Nagasaki, not simply the concentration camps—the Holocaust—but also the everyday violence, part and parcel of the very state and states that Arnold had been putting forward, the European violence and brutal subjugation of colonized persons. Also it has to do with issues of identity, what Paulo Freire has called "conscientization" in new self-perception, in which persons no longer view themselves as objects of history, but rather as subjects of history, willing to put forward their own selves and bodies to reconstruct a new nation. And, of course, ironically appealing to the old European ideology of nationalism to channel their utopian energy. This long-festering underside of modernity, this is not only within European colonies but also with the United States itself—those who for the most part bore the social cost of what Europe understood progress to be, what Europe understood monumental culture to be, what Europe understood order to be.

But, the empire begins to strike back. The impetuous

Decentring Europe

ferocity of moral outrage that motors this process is best captured by Frantz Fanon in his 1961 classic, *The Wretched of the Earth*, published a year after he died at the young age of 36. Fanon from Martinique moves to Paris and then Algeria. He tells us how decolonization which sets out to change the order of the world is obviously a program of complete disorder. Enough dialectical reversal of our normal conception of order on the one hand, and the acknowledgement of the way disorder is part of the process to show the degree to which disorder rests upon a disordering of those beneath—not at the bottom, but beneath—the societies and empires. Decolonization, Fanon says, is the meeting of two forces, opposed to each other by their very nature, which in fact owe their originality to that sort of encounter which results from, and is nourished by, the situation in the colonies. The first encounter was marked by violence in their existence together, that is to say, the exploitation of the native by the settler was carried on by dint of a great array of bayonets and cannons. And decolonization is therefore the need for a complete calling into question of the colonial situation. If you wish to describe it precisely, you might find it in the well-known words, "The last shall be first, and the first, last." Decolonization is the putting into practice of this sentence. The naked truth of decolonization invokes for us bullets and blood-stained knives which emanate from it, for if the last shall be first, it will only come to pass after a murderous and decisive struggle between the two protagonists. Of course, Fanon is linked to a Manichean discourse in this regard, and we can be quite critical of it. But the most important point is the degree to which this long-festering scent of denial and deep degradation had been articulated. Fanon's strong words still describe the feelings and thoughts between the occupying British army and colonized Irish in Northern Ireland, or the occupying Israeli army and colonized Palestinians in the West Bank and Gaza Strip, the Polish army and colonized Polish peoples in Poland, the South African army and colonized black South

Africans, Japanese police presence in Korean communities [in Japan], Russian armies vis-à-vis colonized Armenia—we could go on and on and on. For so many human beings that still live, in fact, within this intersection, within this encounter, in which violence is really at the very edge of how they interact with the model—no buffers, as it were, for the cultural critical discourse given the highly mediated associations between civil societies we experience as humanistic intellectuals. Of course, there were intellectuals, be it Havel in Czechoslovakia, or be it Dennis Brutus in South Africa, and so forth, who have had a much closer experience of what it is to be at the edge of that group—reality. And in the same way, of course, many Afro-Americans and indigenous people in the United States have that close relationship with the repressive apparatus of the state—that close and ugly relationship.

During the late fifties, sixties, and early seventies, these decolonized sensibilities fanned and fueled the civil rights movement, the black power movements, the student anti-war movement, the feminist, gay, and lesbian movements, and this witnessed a shattering of the previous male WASP cultural homogeneity and the collapse of the short-lived liberal consensus. And this, of course, is part of our own moment, the ideological polarization, the racial polarization, the class polarization that comes as a result of a concerted response to this upsurge, this insurgency that took place from 1955 in December, beginning in Montgomery, up until and after the murder—April 4, 1968—of King, with its current ambiguous legacy for both African Americans and Latino and Latina Americans.

Keep in mind that Jamie goes to Yale in the early seventies. Here's that first generation of ruling-class institutions that allow highly talented black folk to attend (Du Bois's PhD was in 1896 and he couldn't think about teaching at Harvard and Yale). Jamie was part of that generation; Professor Henry Louis Gates Jr. was part of that generation; I'm part of that generation; you're talking about a host of others, which means we're riding the tide of decolonizing sensibilities that, by means of organization and mobilization and politicization of the populace under the leadership of people like King, Jr. and a host of others, bring power and pressure to bear on these institutions. And, hence, new kinds of unprecedented opportunities—discursive, political, ideological, existential—begin to present themselves, in a similar trail, of course, for Latinos and Latinas, for Native Americans, and for American women. The entry yields intensive intellectual polemics and inescapable polarization. These polemics and polarization focus principally on the silences and the blindnesses and the exclusions of the male WASP cultural homogeneity and its concomitant notions of the canon. In addition, these critiques promoted three crucial processes that have affected the life and the mind of the country. First was the appropriation of travelling theories of postwar Europe, and this is part of the irony of this moment: that given the McCarthyite suffocation of so much intellectual life in America as it relates to progressive social change, the younger generations had to look to a devastated Europe that was trying to understand its decline in terms of difference as it had been then decentered by the colonized peoples. And you get the kind of radical skepticism of a deconstructive move coming from an Algerian Jewish person who was born as a French colonial subject, but as a special kind of French colonial subject, given the intimacy between Algeria and the French empire. But when I talked to Jacques Derrida it was very clear that he doesn't see a possibility of the decolonization process and, hence, all he can do is try to unsettle the binary oppositions on which the dominant Western cultures rest, with very little possibility of mobilization and organization and so forth. But the skepticism becomes a way of creating openings, even though it's very difficult to make moves in that regard. Then the feminists come along, and the blacks will come along, and say, look, we've got movement. Serious movement here, not just a matter of talking about difference and heterogeneity, but difference and heterogeneity as a matter of concrete embodiment in a certain political direction. It's not just a matter of being accused of being a metaphysician of presence, but trying to change the world. But the charge is very important because of course skepticism is, as Stanley Cavell has taught us, something that never goes away. This link toward the tragic is something that never goes away, but is never concluded—it is always a challenge for those whose backs are against the wall.

But the travelling theories did come. Publishing houses made money, but it also provided a new internationalization of the discourse—the Frankfurt School, Althusser, Gramsci, and on and on—an opening, a crucial opening. But still narrow in the sense of being Eurocentric, still narrow in the sense of not really radically interrogating the context in which these theories emerged as responses to their moment. What were the aims of the appropriate French theory, given the anti-Hegelian moment in France, given the collapse of Marxism at that time, given the devastation of the French Communist Party at that time, given the refusal to say anything about Arab guest workers at that time, and so forth and so on? These kinds of radical interrogations haven't even taken place at the moment. But the important point is that it was an attempt to fuse these versions of transgressive modernisms with what was perceived to be the decline in Marxist, post-Marxist, left politics in the European moment. All interesting enough, but the European figures shun the term postmodernism for the most part, and yet still see themselves deployed in such a way that in the American context they become exemplars of it.

The second moment I want to put forth, now coming to an end here, is the recovery of the revision of American history in light of the rule of those who had been excluded—the workers, the women, African Americans, Native Americans, Latino/a Americans, gays and lesbians, and so forth. I want to argue that this is probably the most important moment. The reason is that if we want to make an historicist turn, then we've really got to come to terms with historiographical practice. We can't make gestures through historicism without understanding what are the new developments and tendencies in present-day historiography. It means reading the Genoveses, reading the Eric Foners, reading the John Blassingames, reading the Paula Giddings, and so forth. It means a certain retooling has to take place for those who have been shaped by the Arnoldian models—by the Eliot and the Trilling-like models—not that there aren't elements there that aren't very important, but the retooling has to take place, and it has to take place in relation to this recovery and recuperation that has been going on. This doesn't mean that we're uncritically accepting, but we have to come to terms with a third moment which has to do with the impact of forms of popular culture, on highbrow literate culture—of television, of film, of music, and of sports. What is the significance, for example, of the fact that in the United States you have, for the most part hegemonic, two forms of cultural activity that have been created by non-middle class persons; namely, black music, on the one hand, and athletics on the other? What is the significance of that in terms of our perceptions of culture? How can we begin to get at these forms in such a way that we're not only critical, but also acknowledging of the internal dynamics at work? What does it mean for these to become hegemonic at particular moments in capitalist society, shaping the identities of those who do not come under the academic purview, and many of those who do? And those who do come under the purview are usually running from it. Why? Because we know that popular culture has been associated with anti-intellectualism that tends to suffocate the life of the mind, and we're trying to preserve critical intelligence in a society that is suffocated by money-making, business operations, and so forth and so on. Very important questions, it seems, and I don't have any definitive answers, as you can imagine. But these are the kinds of questions, again, that James Snead was raising. I recall, I was asked actually to give a lecture on black film at the Whitney Museum in 1984. I knew absolutely nothing about black film, but it's not that uncommon for me to be asked to lecture on something about which I know nothing. That's part of the circulation of the very few black intellectuals in American society, so I refused to go. And I asked Jamie, "Do you know anything?" And Jamie said, "Well, I'm not sure, Cornel." And I said, "Well, I'll tell you what, why don't you go for me." And Jamie did go. And I did not go with him, but I'm told he gave a marvelous lecture. And thank God, from then on he began to move into black film—film in general, but black film especially. He linked up with the *LA Times*, and began to write criticism there, and has written a magisterial text that will be published. We all anxiously await that. But this move into popular culture and trying to keep track of black agency, full of resistance at the level of popular culture, is something that is very important.

After 1973, the end of the American century—the deep crisis of the international world economy, the American slump in productivity, the challenge of OPEC nations in North Atlantic monopoly of oil production, increasing competition in the high-tech sectors of the economy from Japan and West Germany, and the growing fragility of international debt structures of Third World nations—the United States entered the period of waning self-confidence, a period compounded, of course, by Watergate and a contracting economy. The economic boom was over. As the standards of living for the middle classes declined, along with runaway inflation, the quality of living for most fail due to escalating unemployment and underemployment and crime. Secular neo-conservatism and religious conservatism emerge with power and potency. Traditional cultural values are used primarily against feminist gains. That is the groundwork of the era in which we live. And issues of nation and class and gender and race and empire now to come back with power. Hirsch can talk about this in terms of what it means to be a citizen of an empire, to have a certain kind of knowledge, and so he trots out the history of that empire; it's no accident what he excludes—it's predictable what he excludes. Because you don't need what he excludes if you're going to be a responsible citizen in that empire, given his perception of what that empire is, and what its ends and aims are. Postmodernism has to be understood in light of this cultural context of heterogeneity and plurality and academic dissensus, given the historical and social forces at work that I've sketched. In the political context, this is what the market means: the very important production of styles and products for quick consumption and lucrative careers; and the expansion of the professional-managerial class, the degree to which the academy comes to be more and more shaped by the business culture and our students go off into communications and business and medicine, so that, low or high, humanistic studies seem to be outside of where the real action is going on. And for those of us who are left holding the bag, it still is important to read these novels, it still is important to read this criticism, even though we find ourselves undergoing commodification as intellectuals and find our discourses undergoing reification in terms of our ability to communicate. And there's the difficulty of having any organic linkages with any institutions in civil society, like churches and synagogues and mosques and trade unions, and other intermediate associations that have some link to the outside of the academic orbit in which we find ourselves. I'm talking structurally, I'm not talking just about individuals and individual willed volition and so forth. I'm talking about ways in which persons are inscribed within certain structures.

Where does this leave us? It leaves us, I think, very much where Jamie was going, which is to say, it leaves us to talk about traditions of resistance, to talk about holding on to the possibility of social movement and social momentum and social action at a time when it's now unpopular; indeed, when it is very difficult even to imagine, very difficult to imagine, given the larger international constraints in which it seems as though social democracy is the best that anybody can do—in Europe, in the Second World, in the Soviet Union, as well as in the Third World—given the protracted character of the decolonization process, and, of course, its association with the bureaucratic bourgeoisie in these nations, and the butchery of so much of the bureaucratic bourgeoisie in the Third World nations in Africa and Latin America and in parts of Asia—much of Asia one should say. And so it seems to me that the role is going to be one in which we still hold on to some of the precious ideals of rational discourse, democracy, freedom, liberty, and equality. But these notions are read dialectically—they're expanded, they're enriched, they're deepened, they're broadened such that they provide a vision to put forward, such that they yield a courage that has to be mustered in time. Our role as intellectuals remains one that fundamentally links the life of the mind, the best of the life of the mind, to the best of organized forces for social change, even in this conservative moment in which we find ourselves.

But long live the legacy of James Snead. I know I will never, ever forget what he's meant to me—his joy, his laughter, his intelligence, and I'm sure the same is the case for you all here in Pittsburgh. Thank you.

The Black Underclass and Black Philosophers

I want to begin by raising the question of what it means to talk about the black underclass from the vantage point of being a black philosopher. It means then that we have to engage in a kind of critical self-inventory, a historical situating and positioning of ourselves as persons who reflect on the situation of those more disadvantaged than us even though we may have relatives and friends in the black underclass. We have to reflect in part on what is our identity as both black intellectuals, as black philosophers, and more broadly as academicians within the professional-managerial class in U.S. advanced capitalist society. We also must be cognizant of the kind of impact postmodern culture, the culture of this society, is having upon our perceptions, our discourses, our perspectives. Then I'll move to the contemporary discourse on the black underclass. And I'll put forward some theses regarding why I think the black underclass finds itself in the predicament and plight that it is, while highlighting the issue of culture and the way in which culture is linked to institutions and structures. I'll end by saying a few words about what can be done.

Let me begin by raising the issue of the identity of black philosophers. This is an issue that we have been struggling with for over sixteen years when we first came together that lovely evening at Tuskegee Institute in 1973. I want to wax nostalgic about this. It is an issue that all of us have had to come to terms with. What does it mean to be a philosopher of African descent in the American empire? This raises the question of what is our relation to the discipline of philosophy. What is our relation to the dominant paradigms and perspectives in that discipline? Analytic philosophy? Continental modes of philosophizing? To what degree are we willing to transgress these paradigms? What kinds of consequences follow therefrom given the fact that the reward structure of the discipline is such that to transgress means then that we will be marginalized? Now I want to argue that in fact to talk about philosophy in relation to the black underclass means that we have a conception of philosophy that is inexplicably bound to cultural criticism and political engagement. And what I mean by this is that first we begin with a historicist sensibility. And by historist sensibility I mean that we do things that our colleagues find often times very difficult to do which is to read history seriously and voraciously.

Secondly, it means that we engage in an interdisciplinary or even dedisciplinizing mode of knowledge. And what I mean by this is traversing and cutting across the disciplinary division of knowledge inscribed within the universities and colleges, or to radically call into question the very existence of the disciplines themselves. To dedisciplinize means that you go to wherever you find sources that can help you in constituting your intellectual weaponry. This means it is going to be very difficult to obtain tenure in a philosophy department by doing this kind of thing. And all of us have had to struggle with this. This is a serious issue of how, in fact, we remain engaged in our discipline while also radically calling various aspects of it into question if not the whole thing. And having to deal with the marginal status as if you are not "philosophers," or "serious philosophers," "rigorous philosophers," "precise philosophers." And this is not in any way peculiar to black philosophers. This is true for a number of philosophers who called into question in serious ways the dominant paradigms. But black philosophers, I think especially, have been prone to this kind of perception and treatment. If one begins with a historicist sensibility, if one begins with an interdisciplinary or dedisciplinizing orientation, it means also then that one begins to talk about the *worldliness* of one's philosophical project. Here, I of course borrow a term from Edward Said's work, *The World, the Text and the Critic*. In my worldliness, it means you acknowledge quite explicitly the partisan, partial, engaged character of one's own work. Now of course, the immediate charge is that you engage in politicized forms of knowledge. The more charitable reading is you are simply explicit about your values. You're explicit about your political commitment and yet you believe in a critical dialogue and hope that others will be as explicit and unequivocal as to where they stand in relation to their values and political perspectives. But if we take seriously historicist sensibility with dedisciplinizing modes of knowledge and the worldliness of what one is doing, then I think it no accident that we would find ourselves reflecting on something like the black underclass and thereby using tools that have not been bequeathed to us by philosophy departments. Instead we look to cultural criticism, to sophisticated historical work, and to social theory.

Now when we then make the shift to reflection on the black underclass, we begin by reflecting on where we are and what authorizes the claims that we make about the black underclass. Why? Because we know that we are specially for the most part, and certainly socially, distant from the very object that we are constituting as an object of investigation, namely, brothers and sisters who are locked within the black underclass plight. Now, it means then where are we socially? Where are we in regard to class? Where are we culturally? What has been the impact of the degree to which we have been acculturated and socialized into the culture of critical discourse, or the academic subculture? What kinds of values and sensibilities have shaped our socialization given where we come? Many of us do indeed come from working class origins, some underclass origins, some rural black working class origins, and so forth. And what kind of new animal has been constituted in this black philosopher given these origins and given the acculturation? Now I am not arguing that one has to be autobiographical in this regard. But it seems to me before we even begin to talk about one's identity as a black philosopher, one's agency as a black philosopher, we must ask: Who are we speaking to? Who are we writing to? And who in any way holds us accountable? Is it the profession? In part it must be the profession if we are going to be a part of the profession. But is it solely the profession? And if it is more than the profession, then who else is it? Is it the black intellectual community that cuts across disciplines? So to raise these kinds of questions means that we engage in a kind of critical self inventory. Where does that take us? I want to put forth three basic claims about this.

First, I want to argue that we find ourselves in many ways marginalized not solely by white philosophers or mainstream philosophers, but we find ourselves marginalized also because we are humanistic intellectuals. And humanistic intellectuals in general are being marginalized in our society. They are being marginalized by the *technical* intellectuals, e.g. physicists, computer scientists, et. al., because they receive most of the resources from the huge private enterprises and from the state and from the military industrial complex that flows from the nation state. Why? Because the products they provide, of course, are quite useful for society as deemed so by their supporters.

Secondly, as humanistic intellectuals we find ourselves marginalized because middle brow journalists have much more visibility and saliency than we do in the academy. And by middle brow journalists I mean those who work for *Time*, for *Newsweek*, for *Atlantic Monthly*, for *Harper's*, and others who have a large constituency or at least a large audience. And so the consequence in part is that we find ourselves talking more and more to one another hoping that this will serve as a way of sustaining our sense of identity as academic humanists who often feel as if we are becoming antiquated and outdated.

Thirdly, I think in addition to this issue of marginalization is the one of demoralization. And by demoralization I mean the crisis of purpose among black intellectuals in general and black philosophers in particular. I think the recent work of Alan Bloom on the right and Russell Jacoby's book, *The Last Intellectuals,* on the left, are quite reflective of this struggle of crisis of purpose among humanistic intellectuals. On the one hand the loss of public intellectuals, the loss of those academicians who can actually intervene into the larger conversation that affects the destiny of large numbers of persons such as the issue of the black underclass. But on the other hand, it is also reflective of the fact that we find our jobs more and more alienating as we are more and more servicing an upper slice of a labor force that tends to put less and less premium on humanistic studies. So that Pascal begins to displace French as a language—Pascal computer language. So that reading Plato and Aristotle becomes seemingly ornamental and decorative rather than substantive and engaging. It's nice to know a little Plato you can invoke at a cocktail party when you're off relaxing and not making money. But there's no sense that what's at stake might be your very life, as Socrates and many others believed. And this is true at large because while we're in a culture in which the literary is in fact being marginalized *vis-à-vis* the oral by means of the mass media, by means of film, by means of television, by means of radio, not just the oral but of course it's the audio and the visual that I'm talking about. And for those of us who are still intellectuals of the book, it's nice to run into other people who are reading the same books because there are not that many around anymore. And we might think that John Rawls is really so very, very important as I think he is. But we also see the degree to which Rawls finds himself as a towering figure, the last liberal political theorist, as someone who has to be translated in broader ways so that the relevance and pertinence of what he has to say is translatable given the kind of business culture, the business civilization of which we are a part. Now, I think this is especially so in the last twenty years where the hotel civilization—I love that phrase that Henry James invoked in which you get the fusion of the security of the family and the uncertainty of the market—both profoundly private activities, private institutions often distrustful of the common good and the public interest, but more and more serving as the very model of what our culture looks like. And when we then make the shift to the second moment of my presentation which has to do with this discourse on the underclass, we see in fact that the culture of consumption, which is to say the culture of advanced capitalist American society, more and more is the culture that evolves around the market, around buying and selling, around a process of commodification that tends to undermine values, structures of meaning in the name of the expansion of buying and selling, in the name of the procuring profit.

Now this is indeed more than a challenge. I think it is a highly dangerous situation. Why so? It's dangerous because in a market culture in which commodification holds sway over more and more spheres of human life, one sees an addiction to stimulation as the requisite for the consumerism which helps keep the economy going. And, therefore, it tends to undermine community, undermine links to history and tradition, undermine neighborhoods, undermine even qualitative relations since the very notion of commitment becomes more and more contested and bodily stimulation becomes a model for human relations. We see it in the employment of women's bodies in dehumanized ways and in the advertising industry. We see it of course in the sitcoms that tend to evolve around orgiastic intensity. Crack is quite exemplary in this regard. Crack is indeed the postmodern drug because it is the highest level of stimulation known to the human brain. It is ten times more than orgasm, an expression of a culture that evolves around the addiction to stimulation. And stimulation becomes the end and aim much more so than the means, yet the means is the very sphere in which human relations, human community, human traditions, are linked to human history, especially traditions of resistance.

The Black Underclass & Black Philosophers 149

Now what has that to do with the black underclass? It has much to do with the black underclass. Because when we look at the black underclass we see on the one hand a qualitative fissure in the history of people of African descent in this country. Now what I mean by this is, that roughly between 1964 and 1967 black neighborhoods underwent qualitative transformation and the qualitative transformation that they underwent had much to do with the invasion of a particular kind of commodification, namely the buying and selling of a particular commodity—drugs. Now whether it's conspiratorial or not there's no doubt that black communities have fundamentally changed. For the first time we have the disintegration of the *transclass character* of black communities in which different classes live together. So the attempt to sustain the basic institutions of black civil society, family, church, fraternity, sorority, beauty shop, barber shop, shopkeeper, funeral parlor, that used to be in place and served as the infrastructures that transmitted the values and sensibilities to notions of self-respect and self-esteem still had some possibility of distribution across the black community could take place. On the one hand, it is certainly true that, as was talked about this morning, the legacy of 244 vicious and pernicious years of slavery still has its impact on the black psyche. What I mean by this is that the *natal* alienation, the loss of ties at birth of ascending and descending generations, a loss of ties to both predecessor and progeny has certainly created an airborne people, a dangling people, a people who must forever attempt to acquire their self-identity, and self-image in a positive way as they are bombarded with negative ones.

To live for 244 years with no legal standing, no social status, no public worth, only economic value means then that the issue of self-identity remains central. Garvey understood this very well. It's still an issue today I want to suggest. So that the issue of self-doubt, especially among the middle class, issues of self-contempt among large numbers of black folk, a self-hatred, a self-affliction, a self-flagellation, all of these still remain crucial issues in black America, but you can imagine what the legacy of slavery, and the legacy of *natal* alienation is when it intersects with a culture of consumption in which addiction to stimulation becomes the only means by which a vitality is preserved by a self in a society which promotes spectatorial passivity and evasive banality. The culture of consumption generates a passivity by means of spectatorial enactment and it generates a sense of deadening such that the self tries to preserve some sense of itself by engaging in some mode of therapeutic release. We get this in sports, in simulated sexuality, the disco culture, in music, and so forth. We engage in some ritualistic practice, going to the Friday night parties, going to church on Sunday, some ritualistic practice for the self to feel as if it is alive, it is vital, it is vibrant. Now you can imagine, given the legacy of slavery mediated with Jim Crowism, second class citizenship, urbanization, all the different stages and phases that black people have been through from 1619 up to the present and then the culture of consumption that begins to become more and more dominant between 1965 and the present.

What this conjecture has produced, I want to argue, is the major challenge presented to black America, to black scholars, black intellectuals, and to black leaders and black people. And the challenge is this: 1) it has produced the highest level of forms of self-destruction known in black history. And these demons which are at work, the demons of meaninglessness, of hopelessness, a sense of nothingness conjoined with the institutional and structural marginalization of large numbers of black people, though not all (because there is a black working class majority we should not overlook, even a black prosperity among a selective slice of the black middle class, including a few of ourselves owing to the struggle of those in the 60s). But, for the most part, it has produced the highest level of self-destruction known to black people since we arrived. And the reason why is because for the first time there are now no longer viable institutions and structures in black America that can effectively transmit values like hope, virtue, sacrifice, risk, of putting the needs of others higher or alongside those of oneself. And in the past, when you've looked at black colleges in which every Sunday they were forced to sit in those pews and Benjamin Mays would get up and say "You must give service to the race," reminding these black, petty bourgeois students that even as they went out into the world they had a cause, they had an obligation, they had a duty to do something beyond simply that of their own self-interest. Now what they did may have been narrow, and myopic, and short-sighted—but they had an institution that was transmitting that value. That's the point. And it's not just the black school—we can talk about the black church, we can talk about fraternities, we can talk about the whole host of other institutions in black civil society. We no longer have this to the degree that we did in the past and they are being eroded slowly but surely. This is what is most frightening. This is why we get the exponential increase in black suicides between 18 and 35, unprecedented in black history. This is why we get escalating black homicides in which you get some of the most cold-hearted, mean-spirited dispositions and attitudes displayed by black people against other black people as well as non-blacks. It's a breakdown in the moral fabric. Now, conservatives have made much of this point—Glenn Loury, Thomas Sowell, and a host of others have been saying there's something different about black America now, and they highlight the loss of values. But they understand loss of values as simply choices made by individuals as if they are not shaped by the larger structural institutional realities of the cultural consumption. And of course, these larger structures are affecting America as a whole, not just black America. They are affecting America as a whole, but of course the negative consequences tend to be concentrated among those who have lesser access to financial and emotional resources. Now, given this conjecture, the question becomes, how then does one generate institutions, infrastructures? What these institutions and infrastructures did was produce certain kinds of people, many morally virtuous people, not perfect people, but persons who are willing to sacrifice and struggle. How do you sustain these institutions and infrastructures that can produce certain kinds of people so that traditions of resistance can be sustained, and if possible, even expanded? So that when the hotter moments of American society emerge—which is to say those moments in which new progressive and prophetic possibilities surface—you have institutions and infrastructures that can come together, take advantage of them. And if black people have learned anything in America, it is that America is a profoundly conservative country, even given all of its commitments to experimentation and improvisation. And by conservative, what I mean is, conservative in terms of its unwillingness to give up its racism, its sexism, its homophobia. And therefore, the question becomes when you have a chance to push the movement forth you have to move quickly because the leaders and organizations will be crushed. The CIA and the FBI will move quickly, and therefore you know it's not going to last that long. But in order to seize that kind of opportunity, you have to have the ability to produce individuals who will sacrifice, who will live and die for the movement. And these are not petty issues. Part of the problem in contemporary black America is that there's not a deep enough care, and therefore not a willingness to sacrifice. Now, it may sound like a moralist claim that I'm making, but I am actually trying to make a systemic claim, because it has to do with the relative paucity of institutions and infrastructures that can produce these kind of people and then for these people to actually sacrifice their time and energy to engage in a kind of struggle, as those who came before us had to do in order to produce us. Now, how do you do that? What has that to do with black philosophy? It has much to do with black philosophy. One is that we do the kind of thing that we have tried to do for the last sixteen years. We engage in institution building. So that we can at least keep each other in part accountable, even if we don't see each other as much as we like. This is very important. It's very small, but it's very important. It's significant. Because it means, then, not only are we keeping records of what we do, not only are we trying to sustain the vision, trying to hold each other accountable in terms of our sacrifice, and no longer feel as if the issues that once motivated us, issues of freedom, issues of justice, are no longer salient in our own work.

Now, I'm not talking about censorship. I'm not talking about indoctrination. I'm talking about accountability. And accountability is mediated by means of discussion and dialogue—respectful discussion and dialogue. But it is accountability, nevertheless. Even as we reflect on the black underclass, we can sustain our institutions to keep the discussion going and then to intervene into the larger discussion about the black underclass. We've talked about the work of William Julius Wilson keeping in mind that there has always been a black underclass since the end of slavery. What is significant now is the size of it, the social gravity of it, and the frightening and terrifying responses to it. Again, historical perspective is crucial. What are the ways in which the black underclass's predicament can be enhanced? On the one hand, I think that William Julius Wilson is right; that it is going to be a matter of public policy. That no private institution is either willing and/or able to solve the problem of the black underclass. The only private institutions which have the resources to do so, namely multinational corporations, hardly pay their taxes so you can't expect them to take on a major problem like the black underclass. And the notion of the black middle class—not Wilson's view—as the source of the panacea has to be the biggest hoax ever played on any emerging bourgeoisie in the history of the modern world. No middle class in the modern world has been cast as the source of the resolution of the problems of their ethnic or racial working class and underclass.

First, because they don't have the resources to do it. In addition, we have primarily a *lumpenbourgeoisie*. Which is to say we have no serious economic or business class for the most part. Instead, our businesses tend to be locked within the lower echelons of the entrepreneurial sector of the economy in which the multinational corporate sector is the major controller of resources. So to talk about black business in this way is ridiculous. Mr. Reginald Lewis—the leading black businessman in the country—and Mr. John H. Johnson—the second leading black businessman in the country—are not a part of the first 500 of *Forbes*. So to look to these folk as the solution is comical.

The focus then becomes the public sphere, the contestation for power within the state, and hence the black participation in politics. But in this very conservative moment it does not look good even at a time when the Democratic Party is undergoing, as we know, a very slow decline itself, especially given its association with black folk. So that it becomes highly problematic as to how one talks creditably about politics and policies. It is very clear that there have to be resources in place to enhance the situation of the black underclass. There's no doubt about it. People don't want to talk about money and resources, but it's the first step—not the only step—but it is the first step.

Without broader employment, without the child care requisite for the women who are the majority of the black underclass nurturing their children, without the manpower and womanpower problems there can be no serious talk about resolutions of the black underclass. Just a fact. But in addition, as I noted, it's not just a matter of money, it's a matter of values and sensibility, and morally latent ways of life and ways of struggle. There must emerge a new kind of black leadership, a new kind of black organization and association—or set of organizations and associations—that can bring power and pressure to bear on the powers that be. One cannot talk about enhancing the plight of the black underclass without talking about politics, and to talk about politics is to talk about mobilization and organization. And yet to talk about organization and mobilization means to talk about the paucity of institutions and infrastructures.

This is why things become depressing at times. Because when you look around and see what is in place in the black community as it is undergoing this state of siege, you wonder what can be reinvigorated, let alone created, at an institutional level—not just an individual here, not just a book there, just an article there. These are important, but they're limited. One has to talk organizationally, you see. And I would want to argue that, in fact, presently what Professor Lott was talking about in regard to rap music this morning is pertinent here: the degree to which there is institutional articulation of rap music so that power and pressure can be brought to bear as opposed to just the powerful critique mediated through radio. And what kind of institutional translation is taking place? Very little. What are the conditions under which institutional translation can take place? Very difficult issue. And even the Jackson campaign is no answer to this, because there are no serious infrastructures and institutions in the Rainbow Coalition. It's the coming together of persons every four years in a campaign. It's not a deep rooting of institutions and infrastructure in the black and other communities that can be sustained over time and space.

Part of that has to do with Jackson's own institutional impatience. His refusal to engage in serious infrastructure building is part of the problem. And so presently, I would want to argue, that as black intellectuals and as black activists our reflections on the black underclass are significant because the kind of demystification that has taken place today and will take place tomorrow is important at the intellectual level. I want to affirm this and say this quite emphatically, because we live in an anti-intellectual culture and we have to boldly assert our right to engage in intellectual reflection without it having an overnight payoff. It might be linked to a larger project but it may not have overnight payoff but it must be done. If you're thinking as an intellectual who wants to have effectivity and efficacy even further down the road, then you have to think about ways in which the kind of malaise that so much of black America finds itself in can be met. And I would argue that when we look around the black community, what we see is, on the one hand, a set of prophetic churches and mosques, much of it patriarchal, deeply homophobic, but a link to a black freedom struggle that generates persons who are willing to live and die for struggle. They still produce persons who exude and exemplify what they exult and extol in terms of their values. What else do we see? We see some political organization, some neighborhood blocks or associations. Very important. We see infrastructures in relation to sports, Big Brothers programs, Little Leagues. All these character-building activities that seem minuscule but actually are very important in terms of helping produce certain kinds of persons who are indeed willing to engage in struggle. But that's about it. Even our black colleges, more and more, have been so fundamentally shaped by capitalist values that most of our students are graduating in business and communication. And finding humanistic studies, again, ornamental, decorative, "something I have to take because it's part of a path that old folks used to like but I want to make that money and therefore I'm going to zip through this class and take this business class seriously because I want to get into middle class." That's not just black students, that's students across the board, but it is deeply shaping the values of a whole new generation to whom Malcolm X is Malcolm the Tenth, and Martin Luther King is some kind of cultural icon that has no link whatsoever to everyday lives. What a challenge. That's the impasse and the dilemma that I want to suggest, and I don't have any easy way out other than this institution-building, of which this is, in many ways, an instance, given the sixteen-year history of the dialogue of black philosophers. And there are other such institution-building efforts, but I hope that we are on the wave of such an institution-building activity regulated by an all-embracing moral vision, one that talks seriously of class, of gender, of empire, sexual orientation, one that takes seriously social analysis, the historicist sensibility, the dedisciplinizing orientation, and the worldliness. But also, one that takes seriously praxis, which is to say, life commitment, which is to say, sacrificial commitment. I'm not calling for martyrdom, I'm just calling for sacrifice. But it's very important because to be a member of the professional managerial class tends to mitigate against this very sense of commitment. Do you have to go against it? And it means then the rewards are less. It means then that the status is indeed less even if you are at a ruling class institution like Princeton. It still means that the status has to have less value because what you are about dwarfs that. In regard to this greater cause we can continue to produce persons who cultivate and build on these traditions of resistance, so that when the hot moment comes—nobody can predict the hot moment—our "December 55 moment" comes. These infrastructures and institutions can begin to come alive quickly before the repression sets in. And the repression will inevitably set in, and the attacks will inevitably set in because this is America. And there is a lot at stake in the prosperity of America. Black people understand that. Yet it can be pushed, and progressive white comrades and feminist comrades will help push. And then we will be pushed back and the next generation will have to engage in their own challenge, and we hope the next generation of black philosophers will reflect on how they're going to deal with those human beings of African descent who are unemployed, underemployed, have inadequate health care, housing, education and so on. The battle is perennial; yet each of us in our time must fight.

George M. Fredrickson and the Historiography of Race

If there is one fundamental focus in the first-rate scholarship of George M. Fredrickson, it is the historical significance of racism against human beings of African descent in the modern world. Educated and trained at Harvard—interrupted by a brief three year stint in the U.S. Navy (1957-60)—Fredrickson is now regarded by many as, in the words of the distinguished Yale historian David Brion Davis, "our leading authority on racism, anti-racism, and the racial attitudes of whites."[1] The latter concern—the racial attitudes of American whites—is touched on in a suggestive manner in his fine chapter eight entitled "The Meaning of Emancipation" in *The Inner Civil War: Northern Intellectuals and the Crisis of the Union* (1965) and given its best treatment in his superb book, *The Black Image in the White Mind: The Debate on Afro-American Character and Destiny, 1817-1914* (1971). Both books bear the indelible stamp of the subtle Perry Miller tradition in the history of ideas that puts a premium on the integrity and autonomy of thought-systems while holding social, economic and political forces at arm's length. In his best-known work, *White Supremacy: A Comparative Study in American and South African History* (1981), Fredrickson seized two horns at once—the pioneering approaches of social history and comparative history—and thereby struck a strong blow for a synthetic treatment of racism. This seminal synthesis attempted to preserve the *relative* autonomy of ideologies and cultural practices while highlighting the crucial—though never fully determining—roles of geography, demography and, especially, the economy. In his recent collection of seventeen essays, *The Arrogance of Race: Historical Perspectives on Slavery, Racism, and Social Inequality* (1988), Fredrickson makes explicit his methodological stance—"Weber's pluralistic, multicausal approach," his political orientation ("somewhere on the social-democratic left") and his *moral* ranking of race over class ("I regard racial injustice as a distinctive evil, more heinous than the class inequality found in liberal capitalist societies").[2] For Fredrickson, one must avoid the Scylla of economic determinism that explains racism away and the Charybdis of ahistorical essentialisms that reify racism into primordial attitudes built into human nature, if the full historical significance of racism is to be grasped and its effects resisted.

In this presentation, I shall examine three basic theses put forward in Fredrickson's paper in light of his past and present historical reflections on racism in the modern world. In many ways similar to the work of John Rex in Britain, Fredrickson views racism as a specific case of status consciousness in social hierarchies that ascribe honor and prestige to individuals and groups. This Weberian perspective—based on the varying interactions of class, status and party in Weber's *Economy and Society*—tries to keep track of the relative autonomy of the intellectual, cultural and psychological dimensions of racism in light of changing social, economic and political forces. As Fredrickson rightly notes, there are elective affinities between his Weberian views and that of the Chicago class-and-caste school, e.g. Allison Davis, John Dollard, Hortense Powdermaker and others. What distinguishes Fredrickson from these sociologists (or anthropologists) is his own intellectual origins in the history of ideas *and* his creative response to Marxist historiography in the 1970s, e.g. Eugene Genovese, Barbara Fields, Thomas Holt. In this regard, Fredrickson's first thesis constitutes a kind of halfway house between the idealist historiography of his Harvard training and the contemporary Marxist challenge. It is no accident that he considers the preeminent historian C. Vann Woodward "the Dean of American Historians[3]—for Woodward achieves the same golden mean between idealism and Marxism in a unique *literary artistic* manner.

Fredrickson's second thesis is that a Weberian perspective helps us capture the racist aspects of contemporary coded language, e.g. reverse discrimination, Jewish conspiratorial theories, that do not make genetic or cultural inferiority-claims about people. Since status consciousness based on "race" can be perpetuated by appeals to non-racial-sounding rationalizations, Weber's conception is useful. Fredrickson's thesis is that this conception also is indispensable if we are to account for change in the multiple race-relations across cultures and societies. This account roughly is done in terms of the increase (or decrease) in the political and economic power of racially subordinate groups. He notes: "increases in power affect attitudes and changing attitudes open access to power."[4] Therefore, changes in power relations extraneous to race relations—such as major wars, intense international competition among nations or the globalization of capitalist enterprises—often serve as the major impetus to changes in racial attitudes. Within the U.S. context, such structural changes like deindustrialization and class mobility (highlighted recently by William Julius Wilson and others), lead to the conclusion that growth in the group power of black people is inseparable from reducing class inequality. Hence, Fredrickson's preference for "the path of Martin Luther King, Jr. and Jesse Jackson" over against that of Marcus Garvey, Malcolm X and Harold Cruse—and, we might add, Louis Farrakhan.

My criticisms of Fredrickson's project are as follows: First, that his juxtaposition of Weber and Marx is too rigid. In fact, his own advanced appropriation of Weber is not that far removed from sophisticated Marxist historiography—such as that in Marx's own *Class Struggles in France* or *The 18th Brumaire* or the more contemporary works of Marxists like C.L.R. James, W.E.B. Du Bois, Eric Foner, Raymond Williams or Stuart Hall. Fredrickson affirms this point when he states in his most recent book:

The essays in this volume are written from assumptions

similar to those expressed by Du Bois in 1940 [*Dust of Dawn*]. Class is important, very important, but it is not the whole story, and its invocation does not relieve the historian's responsibility to examine "racial folklore" as "instinct, habit, and thought"... Like Du Bois, I am dissatisfied with approaches that subordinate the race question to the class question...[5]

My claim here is that Fredrickson's use of Weber is primarily a strategy of learning from the Marxist tradition while reducing this tradition to its determinist practitioners and thereby preserving the relative autonomy of ideologies. I fully agree with Fredrickson's anti-reductionist aim—but it can be achieved from within the Marxist tradition. And, I should add, in crucial moments in *White Supremacy*, Fredrickson's explanations look quite Marxist—in its non-reductionist mode. One may ask, what's the big deal here? Why push a self-proclaimed Weberian into the sophisticated Marxist camp?

The answer is twofold. First, academic politics. The Academy gives great legitimacy to Weber—or now his rich and eloquent footnote, Foucault—yet Marx still must buck the professional tide owing to ideological baggage. Second, the more important methodological reason, the sophisticated Marxist tradition requires one to attend not only to "the varieties of white opinion about the status of Blacks"[6] but also to examine black cultural responses to white racist oppression. In other words, a methodological approach that highlights the plight and predicament of oppressed people more easily lends itself to inquiry into their intellectual and existential wrestlings with the racist effects and consequences of white supremacist practices in modernity. Given Fredrickson's own origins in intellectual history, it is striking that this monumental struggle with the full historical significance of racism includes no *thorough* or *concentrated* treatment of black intellectuals or African-American cultural thinkers.[7] In this way, Weber rightly preserves the relative autonomy of ideas, yet unlike Marx he provides little push into the treatment of subaltern cultural ways of life and struggle.

My second criticism of Fredrickson's project is that it contains no substantive psychological or cultural theory to understand the "white mind" or "black mind." There is simply no Sigmund Freud, Frantz Fanon, Otto Rank, Ernest Becker, or Albert Memmi in Fredrickson—no analytical tools to help us get a handle on the complex dynamics of castration, impurity phobias, interracial marriage obsessions, namely, the existential stuff of the lived-experience of race relations. He wonderfully reports, describes, narrates and documents the plethora of race relations, yet he leaves us with little or no psychological or existential insights about the phenomena of racism itself. I suspect this is what David Brion Davis has in mind when he concludes his laudatory review of Fredrickson's book:

> Despite the strengths of Fredrickson's approach, the meaning of race itself remains curiously elusive. To what extent is race an ideological construction? How do we account for a man like [Captain John Gabriel] Stedman, who for years fought black rebels and defended slavery and yet condemned racism as a moral insult to humanity? How could a black Jamaican-born tailor like Robert Wedderburn attract such an enthusiastic following among London's most oppressed and poverty-stricken whites, when in contemporary American cities a similar class of whites rejoiced in burning and looting black homes, schools, and churches...[8]

Grappling with these kinds of questions indeed may fall out of the domain of historiography, but they certainly belong to full-scale efforts to grasp the historical significance of racism.

These queries lead me to my last criticism of Fredrickson's project, namely, the refusal to understand the very black nationalist traditions he rejects—on political and moral grounds—as black efforts to wrestle with the very questions for which he has no responses. For example, I fully agree with his social democratic politics, hence black nationalists warrant serious political and usually moral critique. But these black nationalist responses may provide crucial psychological and existential insights into what it means, what it is like and what it takes to preserve black humanity in the modern West. Such black efforts and insights—severed from black nationalist conclusions—are requisite for black sanity, agency and resistance—the very resistance Fredrickson (and Wilson) rightly view as necessary for group empowerment in coalition politics. In short, the full historical significance of racism in modernity cannot be grasped in its psychological and existential dimensions unless black nationalist movements, institutions and practices are understood as crucial phenomena in which the meaning of race is being elaborated and articulated by those who bear the scars. An analysis of such elaborations or articulations necessitates neither black skin nor black nationalist sentiments, but it does require taking the psychological and existential dimensions of black existence seriously as relatively autonomous phenomena—inseparable from though not identical with the political and economic dimensions of racism.

It is ironic that I conclude charging Fredrickson—the champion of anti-reductionist and anti-determinist history writing—with a backhanded kind of reductionism. Yet it does raise the question as to whether any of us can grasp the historical significance of racism without attending to its psychological and existential dimensions. On this question, neither Marx nor Weber is sufficient —though they are indispensable. Fredrickson's magisterial scholarship helps us raise this question in all its profundity and mystery— even as the scars persist, the damage continues and we wade deeper in the postmodern racial mire.

Notes

1. David Brion Davis, "The Ends of Slavery," *New York Review of Books*, March 30, 1989.

2. *The Arrogance of Race*, p. 7.
3. *Ibid.*, p. 216.
4. Unpublished paper, p. 9.
5. *The Arrogance of Race*, p. 4.
6. *Ibid.*, p. 5.
7. He does provide a fine short reading of Waldo Martin's "The Mind of Frederick Douglass" in *The Arrogance of Race*, pp. 80-88. He is now writing a book on black intellectuals.
8. David Brion Davis, *New York Review of Books, op. cit.*, p. 34.

On Walt Whitman

Walt Whitman is not only America's most original poet; more importantly, he is, in the words of David Thoreau, "the greatest democrat the world has ever seen," His most profound and poignant poems—"Song of Myself," "To Think of Time," "Crossing Brooklyn Ferry," "Out of the Cradle Endlessly Rocking," and his famous homage to Abraham Lincoln, "When Lilacs Last in the Dooryard Bloomed"—enact the heroic endeavor to make and remake a dynamic and empathetic self. They attempt to sing in his words, "the song of a great composite *democratic individual*." Similarly, his prosaic masterpiece of cultural criticism, *Democratic Vistas* (1871) is the landmark text in modern democratic thought. It belongs alongside John Stuart Mill's *On Liberty* (1859), W.E.B. Du Bois's *The Souls of Black Folk* (1903) and John Dewey's *The Public and Its Problems* (1927) as a classic in the defense of individuality and social justice.

What sets Whitman the poet apart from his nineteenth century contemporaries is his uncanny ability to perfect the Wordsworthian revolution of writing poetry based on the spoken language and everyday life. And what sets Whitman the critic apart from his fellow men and women of letters is his enervating faith in democracy as a way of life and mode of being in the world—not simply as a form of governance. It was only Whitman in his day who took up the exciting yet frightening risk of living, thinking and feeling democratically; for him, democracy had deep ontological, existential and social implications.

The unique experience of reading Whitman's poetry is that of a heartfelt presence of intimacy solicited by a powerful voice that fuses soul, mind and body. His poetry resembles an oracular epic that deploys dramatic speech, gesture and tone without any vulgar sense of the didactic and sermonic. Yet it aims to convince and convert as well as to energize and provoke. Whitman's intention is to release the creative powers of his readers to make and remake themselves, just as his poetic style exemplified this creative process in Whitman himself. It is no accident that his artistic models tended to be drawn not from literature but rather the theater, music (especially Italian opera and other popular forms) and, to some extent, charismatic religious rhetoric (of the prophetic sort). He writes as if literature did not exist, with no quotations, no references to any other writers or allusions to the classics or ancients. And he realizes that such writing has to be an extremely self-conscious act of high craftsmanship to achieve this effect—the effect of touching the hearts, moving the souls and changing the lives of his readers.

Like Nietzsche, Whitman associated this effect with life-enhancing self-scrutiny and heightened self-creation. Unlike Nietzsche, Whitman located this effect in the moral and intellectual capacities of common people. Similar to fellow countryman Ralph Waldo Emerson, Whitman believed that every man was a potential Prometheus, a possible Napoleon of the spirit. His democratic faith rests upon the pillars of voluntarism, fallibilism and experimentalism. His kind of voluntarism accented a willful self-making and self-mastery that required great discipline and energy. His kind of fallibilism stressed the Piercean slogan of never blocking the road to inquiry, or, in the words of George Kateb, "Nothing is for keeps." Lastly, his kind of experimentalism promoted an existential risk that wagered on the abilities of common people to control their own individual and collective destinies. In this sense, democracy for Whitman was never a static end in itself, but rather a dynamic means for the cultivation and encouragement of the potentialities and possibilities of unique individuals. In *Democratic Vistas* he states:

> For it is not that democracy is of exhaustive account, in itself. It is that, as we see, it is the best, perhaps only, fit and full

means, formulator, general caller-forth, trainer, for the million, not for grand material personalities only, but for immortal souls. To be a voter with the rest is not so much; and this, like every institute, will have its imperfections. But to become an enfranchised man, and now, impediments removed, to stand and start without humiliation, and equal with the rest; to commence or have the road clear'd to commence, the grand experiment of development, whose end, (perhaps requiring several generations) may be the forming of a full-grown man or woman—that is something...the democratic formula is the only safe and preservative one for coming times.

For Whitman, our present-day capitalist democracies—now in a self-congratulatory mood after the collapse of repressive communist regimes in Eastern Europe—are but initial steps in his adventure of democracy, because too many "impediments," e.g. class, racial and sexual ones, to self-development remain. Hence, his democratic challenge to us still requires a substantive response.

The Legacy of Raymond Williams

Raymond Williams was the last of the great European male revolutionary socialist intellectuals born before the end of the age of Europe (1492-1945). I use this long string of adjectives not to pigeonhole the complex and multiple identities of Williams, but rather to examine and evaluate his grand achievements and incomplete efforts in light of the social crises and political travails of his time. To do honor to him is to keep the legacy of his work and life alive. And to keep this legacy alive is, in part, to keep in view how he made and remade himself—cast and recast his ways of life and ways of struggle—under circumstances (usually adverse circumstances) not of his choosing.

In my brief comments, I shall suggest that the major contribution of Williams to our present-day challenges is not simply that he taught us how to think historically about cultural practices or how to approach political matters with a subtle cultural materialist orientation in a manner that stands head and shoulders above any of his generation. Rather, Williams speaks to us today primarily because he best exemplifies what it means for a contemporary intellectual leftist to carve out and sustain, with quiet strength and relentless reflection, a sense of prophetic vocation in a period of pervasive demoralization and marginalization of progressive thinkers and activists. His career can be seen as a dynamic series of critical self-inventories in which he attempts to come to terms with the traditions and communities that permit him to exercise his agency and lay bare the structural and personal constraints that limit the growth of those traditions and communities.

These critical self-inventories take the form of powerful cultural histories and fictions and often persuasive cultural critiques of the European past and present, in order to create new possibilities for left thinkers and activists. In this sense, Williams' deep historical sensibilities were grounded in a *prospective* outlook that never loses sight of human struggle against transient yet formidable limits. Whatever the intellectual fashion of the day—from F.R. Leavis to Louis Althusser, Jacques Lacan to Michel Foucault—Williams remained wedded to subtle humanist notions of struggle and hope found in traditions and communities. In fact, one of his distinctive contributions to Marxist theory was to revise the understanding of class conflict—inseparable from but not identical with class struggle—by highlighting how, in relatively cold moments in human societies, class conflict is mediated through social, cultural or educational changes that insure the muting of class struggle. Like Gramsci, Williams injects notions of contestation and incorporation into the understanding of class conflict while reserving class struggle for that hot moment in societies in which structural change becomes a conscious and overt engagement of forces. Again his aim is to tease out the concrete and credible lines of action for progressive thinkers and activists.

Williams's creative attempts to make and remake himself by means of critical self-inventories occurred on three major terrains. On the *ideological* terrain he had to navigate between the deformation of socialism in the names of Stalinism and fabianism. The former was a vicious autocratic statism that repressed civil society and regimented its citizens—an undeniable affront to Williams's socialist democratic values; the latter—a naive gradualism which assumed that the enemy was a mere party rather than "a hostile and organized social formation"—an unacceptable conclusion given Williams's historical materialist analysis.

On the *academic* terrain, Williams sought to counter conservative traditions of thinking about culture represented by T.S. Eliot and F.R. Leavis by refining crude left reflections about the relation of culture and democracy, art and socialism. And on the *political* terrain, Williams sought to reconceive the notion of revolution such that cultural practices were neither overlooked nor viewed in a simplistic manner. The point was not only that culture—including popular culture—was to be viewed as a crucial site of struggle, but also that the very ways in which culture was understood in capitalist societies had to be demystified and transformed. In reading Williams's masterpieces, *Culture and Society* (1958); *The Long Revolution* (1961); *The Country and the City* (1973); and *Marxism and Literature* (1977) we get a sense of the evolution of his own democratic socialism, cultural materialism and revolutionary activism.

Yet, in all honesty, what also attracted me to Williams's work was his refusal to sidestep the *existential* issues of what it means to be a left intellectual and activist—issues like death, despair, disillusionment and disempowerment in the face of defeats and setbacks. He understood on a deep level that revolutionary activity was as much a matter of feelings as facts, of imagination as organization, of agency as analysis. Therefore he highlighted what most left thinkers tend to ignore: *the need for vision and the necessity of linking vision to visceral forms of human connectedness.* His preoccupation with vital traditions and vibrant communities, sustaining neighborhoods and supportive networks, reflected his sensitivity to how ordinary people in their everyday lives are empowered and equipped to deal with defeats and setbacks. In his six novels as well as his often overlooked gem, *Modern Tragedy* (1966), Williams explores the highly mediated links between human struggle, bonding and place. This exploration is neither an extraneous affair of nostalgic yearning for the Welsh *Gemeinschaft* of his youth, nor an escapist inclination to displace the political for the personal. Rather he is grappling with one of the central problematics of our moment: how to articulate visions, analyses and forms of praxis that anchor socialist politics to the contingent constructions of identities of degraded and downtrodden peoples. These new identities—often associated with the "new" social movements of women, people of color, formerly colonized persons, gays, lesbians and greens—emerge from various cultural politics of difference that put a premium on bonding and place, common experiences in time and similar situations in space. In the late sixties, Williams began to visibly struggle with his Welsh European identity—as manifest in his novel *The Fight for Manod* (1979). Yet it is precisely at this point where Williams's grand example falls short; that is where he appears more a creature of his time than a creator who links us to the coming epoch. Edward Said has made this point in terms of Williams's "relative neglect of the affiliation between imperialism and English culture" (*Nation*, March 5, 1988). I would add that though Williams provides indispensable analytical tools and historical sensibilities for reflections on empire, race, color, gender and sexual orientation, the relative silences in his work on these issues bear the stamp of his own intellectual and existential formation, and his later attempts to accent a Welsh nationalist identity within his socialist project bear this out.

Those of us born and shaped after the end of the age of Europe must begin with the legacies of the European empire—legacies of deeply inscribed white supremacist and male capitalist metropoles—as well as with the declining U.S. and Soviet empires. And as expanding cultures of consumption slowly erode traditions, communities, neighborhoods and networks, new cultural configurations must be created if any substantive sources of struggle and hope for fundamental societal change can be preserved and sustained. In this regard, the last problematic Williams gallantly yet inadequately confronted becomes our major challenge. And if we plan to meet it, we must do so by, in part, standing on his shoulders, and hope we meet it as well as he did others.

Jeffrey Stout's
Ethics After Babel

Jeffrey Stout is one of the most penetrating and provocative philosophers on the American scene. He also is the leading moral critic of a pragmatic bent concerned with the relations between secular thought and religious traditions as well as the history of modern Western ethics. In his exciting new book, Stout extends his concerns into the terrain of social criticism. Although he still grapples with the challenges of skepticism, relativism, and nihilism to his own sophisticated historicist perspective, it is clear that the *élan vital* of the text is the role and function of moral discourse in contemporary American society. In my brief response to Stout's fascinating book, I shall highlight what I consider to be the fundamental contribution Stout makes to how we should do our work as cultural critics. This contribution consists of his call for a new mode of social criticism—a mode I shall dub *improvisational criticism.*

Stout uses such phrases as "creative bricolage," "eclectic and pragmatic moral bricoleur," and "moral bricolage" to describe his conception of cultural criticism. He is well aware that these phrases must be understood contextually; that is, relative to the available traditions or fragments of traditions vital and vibrant in this particular moment in American society, namely, liberalism, civic republicanism, and religious traditions. What interests me here is not so much that Stout does not provide us with a fully elaborated account of what strands and streams of our traditions could and should be brought together in order to bring "into focus the resources that liberal society makes available for its own transformation." The concrete cases he treats give us some sense of how a subtle improvisational moral critic melts icy cold binary oppositions and breaks down rigid distinctions for the purposes of capturing the complexity and concrete character of an issue. Rather, I would like to note the degree to which Stout's version of cultural criticism is an advance beyond Richard Rorty's neo-pragmatic defense of the Enlightenment and Alasdair MacIntyre's neo-Aristotelian trashing of the Enlightenment. This Rorty-MacIntyre debate—reproduced in various ways between liberals like Ronald Dworkin and communitarians like Michael Sandel, upbeat critical theorists like Jürgen Habermas and downbeat civic republicans like Robert Bellah—signifies a crucial shift for contemporary pragmatic thinkers such as Stout toward explicit engagement in social and political philosophy. Stout's improvisational criticism is the most significant attempt I know to advance the dialogue between neo-pragmatic liberals and neo-Aristotelian (or neo-Hegelian) anti-liberals.

The major strength of Stout's project is that it mediates the clashing perspectives by means of *immanent criticism*. It proceeds by highly sympathetic and charitable readings of both viewpoints, then teases out internal inconsistencies, blindnesses, and contradictions, all in order to disclose common ground between supposedly antagonistic positions. This approach is Socratic rather than Hegelian—and thoroughly dialectical. So, there is no grand third moment or emergent synthesis with elements of both positions intact, but rather a mutual recognition by both sides of fallacious assumptions and convergent values that bond them. The outcome is that the limited lenses through which they viewed each other are removed. This removal does not result in epistemic lucidity, but rather in possible convergence and potential solidarity. Stout's treatment of the widely-heralded liberalism/communitarianism debate is exemplary in this regard.

Stout's notion of moral bricolage—or improvisational criticism—is a much richer notion than the garden variety pragmatic idea of experimentalism and the relativist rendering of eclecticism. Stout's improvisational criticism is a telos-ridden, ideology-laden activity that requires thorough interrogation of prospective teleological and ideological candidates—yet, it is mindful of the inescapable character of teleology and ideology in our ethical stances. It thereby sidesteps the common criticism of certain pragmatic ideas of experimentalism in which technique tends to predominate over ends. Similarly, Stout's improvisational criticism puts a premium on rigorous thought, logical reflection, and warranted assertability. Therefore, it shuns any forms of sloppy thinking that settle for vast cathartic variety at the expense of high *rational* quality. In this way, it jettisons relativistic versions of eclecticism.

The major weakness of Stout's improvisational criticism is that it runs the risk of being so preoccupied with arriving at the golden mean between extremes that it often slights structural deficiencies—in rhetorics, cultures, societies—that reinforce the very polarizations he wants to mediate. This weakness is rooted in the pivotal terms in Stout's discourse. These terms—"crisis," "impasse," "malaise," "dramatic resolution"—are part of a discourse centered on the *therapeutic* and the *conversational*. The influential figures here are Wittgenstein and Rorty. The problem is that Wittgensteinian and Rortian metaphors are not particularly useful for serious social criticism. The shift from epistemic argumentation and intellectual history to cultural criticism renders these crucial terms suspect. The content and character of an epistemic crisis, conversational impasses, or discursive malaise is quite different from a social crisis, societal impasse, or political malaise. In one sense, Stout is aware of this point. Yet, his social criticism often proceeds as if the key terms in his discourse have adequately grappled with issues of structural deficiencies, operations of social power, cultural capital, or economic constraints. This is why his ingenious arrival at common ground is persuasive at the dialogic level of philosophical reflection, but at most only plausible at the concrete levels of power and politics. Needless to say, he would have had to write another and different kind of book to do what I request. Yet, a social critic of Stout's talent and ambition must not only go about his work with both eyes open, but also with both hands dirty.

Paulo Freire

Paulo Freire is the exemplary organic intellectual of our time. If Antonio Gramsci had not coined this term, we would have to invent it to describe the revolutionary character and moral content of the work and life of Paulo Freire. It is safe to say that his classic work, *Pedagogy of the Oppressed*, was a world-historical event for counter-hegemonic theorists and activists in search of new ways to link social theory to narratives of human freedom. This complex lineage led Freire to put a premium on dialogue, the construction of new subjects of history and the creation of new social possibilities in history. In contrast to Hans-Georg Gadamer's call for dialogical hermeneutics, or Richard Rorty's charge for edifying conservation, Freire's project of democratic dialogue is attuned to the concrete operations of power (in and out of the classroom) and grounded in the painful yet empowering process of conscientization. This process embraces a critical demystifying moment in which structures of domination are laid bare and political engagement is imperative. This unique fusion of social theory, moral outrage and political praxis constitutes a kind of pedagogical politics of conversion in which objects of history constitute themselves as active subjects of history ready to make a fundamental difference in the quality of the lives they individually and collectively live. Freire's genius is to explicate in this text and exemplify in his life the dynamics of this process of how ordinary people can and do make history in how they think, feel, act and love. Freire has the distinctive talent of being a profound theorist who remains "on the ground" and a passionate activist who gets us "off the ground"—that is, he makes what is abstract concrete without sacrificing subtlety and he infuses this concrete way of being-in-the-world with a fire that fans and fuels our will to be free.

In this way, he adds new meaning to Marx's famous 11th thesis on Feuerbach, "the philosophers have only interpreted the world in various ways; the point, however, is to change it." This new meaning consists of recasting philosophical reflection among subaltern peoples in their everyday life settings and reconceiving of change as the creation of new collective identities and social possibilities in history over against vicious forces of dehumanization. Paulo Freire dares to tread where even Marx refused to walk—on the terrain where revolutionary *love* of struggling human beings sustains faith in each other and keeps hope alive in themselves and history.

Michael Harrington, Socialist

The death of Michael Harrington is the end of an era in the history of American socialism. He was the socialist evangelist of our time—the bearer of the mantles of Eugene Debs and Norman Thomas. Unlike Debs and Thomas, however, Harrington was a serious intellectual. His first book, *The Other America* (1962)—with a boost from Dwight Macdonald's famous review in *The New Yorker*—thrust him into the limelight and prompted the Kennedy Administration's campaign against poverty. His fifteen other books ranged from solid history of Western socialist movements (*Socialism*, 1972), to analysis of advanced capitalist societies (*Twilight of Capitalism*, 1976), to autobiographical reflections (*The Long-Distance Runner*, 1988), to broad pronouncements about the prevailing crisis of Western civilization (*The Politics at God's Funeral*, 1984). Though far from original works, these books guided and inspired many progressives in their struggles for freedom, solidarity and justice.

Like the late Raymond Williams in Britain and the late C.P. Macpherson in Canada, Harrington carved out a vital democratic socialist space between the Scylla of Stalinism and the Charybdis of liberalism. With his early roots in Irish Catholicism he was a Pascalian Marxist who wagered boldly on the capacity of ordinary men and women to create and sustain a socialist future. Harrington was also a socialist in the American grain: experimental in method, moral in motivation and optimistic in outlook. Like Walt Whitman, John Dewey and C. Wright Mills, he believed in the possibility of social betterment by means of creative intelligence, moral suasion and political struggle. Yet he was the first great democratic socialist in the United States to be well read in the Marxist classics (his translation of Georg Lukács's "What Is Orthodox Marxism?" 30 years ago was the first in this country) *and* to have mastered the details of progressive public policy. Endowed with great ambition, talent, discipline and curiosity—but no Ph.D.—he became the shining knight and activist intellectual of the democratic left for nearly three decades.

Harrington was the product of two distinct intellectual subcultures: those of the artistic bohemian radicals (centered at the White Horse tavern in Greenwich Village) and the anti-Stalinist socialists of the late 1950s and early 1960s. The former changed him from a follower of Dorothy Day's Catholic social gospel (after college at Holy Cross, a year at Yale Law School and an M.A. in English at the University of Chicago) into a secular proponent of sexual freedom and racial equality; the latter turned him into a self-styled Marxist with deep democratic sentiments. Both left subcultures were thoroughly New Yorkish and disproportionately Jewish, and thus permeated by intense conversation, bookish knowledge, oppositional outlooks and identification with the oppressed and exploited. Harrington's superb oratorical skills, voracious reading and links with the progressive wing of the labor movement were fundamentally shaped by these subcultures—which are no longer available to young intellectuals. His charisma as a progressive leader and his heritage as a public intellectual bore this particular historical stamp, and reflected as well his good nature and his ability to reconcile opposing people and ideas.

In his last book, *Socialism: Past and Future,* Harrington grapples with the most fundamental questions facing democratic socialists: Is socialism more than "the hollow memory of a passionate youth" or "humankind's most noble and useful political illusion"? Can the socialist ideal once again become credible and desirable, given its heavy "baggage of historic failure" in the form of command economies, bureaucratic authoritarian elites and repressive regimentation of ordinary people in the "actually existing" communist countries? What are the analytical contents, practical socioeconomic arrangements and moral values that define the term "socialism"? Does the term obstruct and obscure the very ideals it purports to promote? What does it mean to be a democratic socialist today?

Harrington's attempt to reply to these pressing questions constitutes not only a re-evaluation of the socialist life he led but also a projection of his legacy. The book was begun the day he was told that he had inoperable cancer and a limited time to live. And the text is vintage Harrington—lucid, candid, tempered yet upbeat. His basic argument is that the hope for human freedom and justice in the future rests upon the capacity of people to choose and implement democratic forms of socialization in the face of "irresponsible," "unthinking" and "unsocial" versions of corporate socialization. Harrington defines corporate socialization as a fusion of Weber's notion of rationalization, or the expansion of bureaucratic hierarchies that impose impersonal rules and regulations in order to increase efficiency, and Marx's idea of commodification, or the globalization of capital. (This takes the form of centralizing corporations that concentrate power and wealth and render people increasingly dependent on market forces to satisfy their needs and desires.) For Harrington, the fundamental choice is not between rigid command economies and "free markets," or between bureaucratic collectivist regimes and capitalist democracies. Rather, the basic choice in the future will be between a democratic, or "bottom-up" socialization, and corporate, or "top-down" socialization. This choice is much more complex than it appears on the surface and is a far cry from the classic Marxist choice between socialism and barbarism posed by Rosa Luxemburg.

First, Harrington's notion of democratic socialization has nothing to do with nationalization or state control of economic enterprises. Nor is it associated with a socialist "negation" of capitalism. Instead, it is a process in which social forces—especially those brought to bear by progressive groups, associations and organizations—try to broaden the participation of citizens in the economic, cultural and political spheres of society and thus control the conditions of their existence. At present these forces are weak compared with those of corporate socialization. Orthodox Marxist-Leninists have made the fatal mistake of reducing democratic socialization to elitist nationalization, creating monstrosities that are neither socialist nor capitalist, neither free nor efficient.

Second, Harrington shows that the reality of corporate socialization can be separated from the rhetoric about "free markets" or the absence of state intervention in the economy. As Reagan and Thatcher illustrated, corporate socialization, despite conservative pieties about "laissez-faire" capitalism, is deeply statist, with its military buildups, socially authoritarian regimentation of the labor force, moral strictures on individual (especially women's) choices, and a debt-financed public sphere.

Third, democratic socialization, in Harrington's view, entails more than workers' participation in investment decisions (including access to relevant knowledge and information) and the use of markets for non-market purposes. It also requires a new culture, a new civilization. Harrington's attempt to define this "new socialism" harks back to the best of the nineteenth century utopian socialists, such as Charles Fourier, Robert Owen and the Saint-Simonians. While Harrington shuns their naïveté, moralism and messianism, he accents their feminist, communitarian and cultural radicalism. He then adds a strong anti-racist and ecological consciousness that calls for a new global civilization in which wealth is distributed more equally and life is lived more meaningfully.

Harrington's project is indeed visionary. Yet he struggles to make it appear to be more than mere fantasy. So he accepts the sacred cow of the present capitalist structure of accumulation—namely, economic growth—and attempts to show how it can be channeled toward qualitative living, not merely quantitative consuming. He proposes replacing the gross national product with a new set of statistics, the qualitative national (and international) product, which would subtract from the GNP environmental degradation, premature death, wasteful packaging and uninformative advertising in order to keep track of the quality of life. Further, Harrington suggests a restructuring of the United Nations and its related economic institutions—such as the World Bank and the International Monetary Fund—in order to transfer resources from North to South and promote cultural differences. He emphatically points out that Third World debt not only forces cutbacks in crucial social services for the countries' poor people but also prevents the South from consuming First World goods—consumption that could fuel economic growth in both North and South. And his trenchant critique of the calculated dependence of the export-led economies of the Four Tigers (Taiwan, South Korea, Hong Kong and Singapore)—the showcase countries for conservative economists—reveals the fragility of the present international economic order. His discussion is extremely relevant to Eastern Europeans clamoring for the "free market"—that is, full integration into the corporate-dominated economic order of the West.

How will democratic socialization come about? How do we radically reform a system while working within it? How can democratic socialist practices be more than a social democracy in which corporate priorities operate within a public sector organized by liberals and managed by bureaucratic elites? And given the fragmentation and casualization of the labor force—the de-skilling and re-skilling of workers due to the automation, computerization and robotization in the workplace—who will be the major agents of social change?

Harrington approaches these questions with candor and caution. First, he assumes that any socialist conception of social change must be epochal, not apocalyptic. He finds it impossible to conceive the triumph of democratic socialization in the next 50 years. Second, he presents Sweden's social democratic order as the major inspiration—not the utopian model or flawless example—for figuring out how to overcome the most inegalitarian effects of corporate socialization. Sweden's policy of "collective capital formation," which links growth to efficiency and democratic management, and solidaristic wage demands that first reward those at the bottom of the labor force fall far short of his vision. Yet they show what can be done when pressure is brought to bear on capital in the interests of social justice and democratic participation. Harrington acknowledges the precious gains achieved by reformers as well as the structural constraints on reform. His notion of "visionary gradualism" is an attempt to walk this tightrope of short-term strategies and tactics and long-term aims.

But is he successful? Does he remain blind to possible new social forces or silent about new strategies for change? It is extremely difficult to know how to measure "success" here. Certainly social movements he did not foresee may emerge. New cleavages in the fragile conservative camp could weaken the right offensive, and structural transformations could threaten the present forms of corporate socialization. Yet it would be unfair to blame Harrington for failure to predict such events.

The major problem I have with Harrington's impressive project is that it remains too far removed from lived experience in advanced capitalist societies. Despite his call for a new culture, he does not discuss the civic terrorism that haunts our city streets; the central role of TV, video, radio and film in shaping the perceptions of citizens; the escalating violence against women, gays and lesbians; the racial and ethnic polarization or the slow decomposition of civil society (families, schools, neighborhoods and associations). There are no reflections in the book about the impact of the plagues of drugs and AIDS on a terrified populace or the entrenchment of jingoistic patriotism and nationalism. Although he invokes Gramsci, Harrington is more interested in the notion of "historic blocs"—coalition politics—

than in the actual operations of hegemony that mobilize people's "consent" (in the forms of indifference or passivity) to the "fate" of corporate socialization. Subtle investigations into such cultural, experiential and existential realities—as intimated in the works of Georg Simmel, Lukács, Walter Benjamin, Siegfried Kracauer and other cultural critics—are needed before democratic socialization can become more than a noble ideal.

Harrington combined many of the best qualities of the old Left and a genuine openness to some of the insights of the New Left. In his life and work, the fist and rose begin to come together. With the historic merger of his organization, the Democratic Socialist Organizing Committee, with the New American Movement in 1982, this unity-in-process, though full of tension, was manifest. His mere presence gave the new group, Democratic Socialists of America, a visibility and legitimacy in progressive circles far beyond its numbers (roughly 7,000).

Because the Left is organizationally weak and intellectually timid relative to its conservative counterparts (it is armed more with journals and gestures than with programs and politicians), it has tended to rely on charismatic spokespersons and insurgent movements. Harrington's death makes this situation more apparent. The splitting of the old and New Lefts from the black, brown, yellow and red lefts—dating back to the mid-1960s—exacerbates the predicament of progressives. This is why Jesse Jackson's Rainbow politics is so refreshing. It is a new multi-racial attempt to channel the inchoate left-liberal sentiments of ordinary people into an electoral campaign of national scope. Yet the legacy of Harrington, as well as those of Martin Luther King Jr., Fannie Lou Hamer and Malcolm X, as well as the efforts of feminists, greens, the Gray Panthers and gays and lesbians, deserves a movement with deeper roots. Jackson's courageous attempt to gain power at the national level is a symptom of the weakness of the Left—a sign that its capacity to generate extra-parliamentary social motion or movements has waned. The best way to keep the legacy of Harrington alive is to go beyond it by building from grassroots citizens' participation in credible progressive projects in which activists see that their efforts can make a difference. In this way, the crucial difference that Michael Harrington made in many of our lives can become contagious.

The Prospects for Democratic Politics: Reconstructing the Lippmann-Dewey Debate

Let me first say I'm delighted to be here. I have never lectured at U.C. Berkeley before. My brother, who is here today, attended U.C. Berkeley and graduated a few years ago. I never had a chance to come back to his alma mater, you see. It's quite moving for me to stand here where he studied, primarily, when he was here, though he also set the mile record for freshmen that first year when he was here, but he primarily studied. Second, I would like to congratulate Bob and Anne and Richard and Steve and William on the text *The Good Society*. I think that it has made a very significant intervention in our public conversation even as it tries to reconstitute that conversation. It brings us together and I look forward to our dialogue both later on this afternoon and tomorrow. I hope it's sharp, I hope it heats up a bit. I like intellectual passion, but mediated by civility and respect.

Let me begin with an epigram:

> I see we had best look our times and lands searchingly in the face like a physician diagnosing some deep disease. Never was there perhaps more hollowness at heart than at present, than here in the United States. Genuine belief seems to have left us. The underlying principles of the states are not honestly believed in for all this hectic glow, these melodramatic screaming, patriotic and jingoistic gestures. Nor is humanity itself believed in. What penetrating eye does not everywhere see through the mask? The spectacle is appalling, we live in an atmosphere of hypocrisy throughout: the men believe neither in the women nor the women in the men. A scornful superciliousness rules. In literature the aim of all the literary critics is to find something to make fun of.

A lot of churches, the most dismal phantasms I know, usurp the name of religion. Conversation is a mass of petty banter. The depravity of the business classes of our country is not less than has been supposed but infinitely greater. The official services of America, national, state, and municipal, in all their branches and departments, except the judiciary, are saturated in corruption, bribery, falsehood and mal-administration. And the judiciary is tainted. The great cities reek with respectable as well as non-respectable robbery and scoundrelism. In fashionable life flippancy, tepid amours, weak fidelity, small aims or no aims at all, resonate the killing of time. In business the one sole object—the all-devouring modern word business—is, by any means, pecuniary gain. The magician's serpent, in the fable, ate up all the other serpents, and money-making is our magician's serpent, remaining today sole master of the field. I say that our new world democracy is so far an almost complete failure in its social aspects, and in really grand religious, moral, literary and aesthetic results. In vain do we march with unprecedented strides to empire so colossal. It is as if we were somehow being endowed with a vast and more and more thoroughly appointed body and then left with little or no soul.

That's Walt Whitman, 1871, *Democratic Vistas*—one of the canonical pillars for any radical democrat like myself. Very important, because I want to reflect today on the prospects for democracy, alluding a bit to the debate between Lippmann and Dewey but focusing primarily on how we talk about sources of hope, tempered hope, but talk about sources of hope for radical democrats in the latter part of the twentieth century. Whitman was writing at a time of national division and cultural delinquency, right after the Civil War. Cultural delinquency: America dealing with its inferiority complex vis-à-vis Europe. But ours is a moment of national decline and cultural decay.

In order to situate, characterize, analyze our moment, we have to go back to 1945. It's a crucial moment in the history of the human adventure, the end of the age of Europe, begun in 1492. Mushroom clouds over Nagasaki and Hiroshima, ugly and incredulous concentration camps in Europe, primarily for Jews, but also some Gypsies, some gays and lesbians, and some communists, and some socialists. 1945. The first new nation steps to the center of the historical stage, the U.S.A. The hotel civilization. The fusion of the market and the home, a quest for the warmth and security of the home but also for that upward social mobility that gives American social structure its relative fluidity vis-à-vis European social structures, but both profoundly privatistic phenomena, distrustful of common good and public interest. In raising the question that E.O. Mathiessen would struggle with all of his life: Is it the case that this new nation would move from a moment of perceived innocence to corruption without a mediating stage of maturity? Keep in mind, 50 million people dead in 1945. Twenty million Russians dead. That would be the alternative empire that would define the American identity. Being American is not to be communist. Negative identity. American soldiers, each life precious, 390,000 dead, which is less than those lost in one battle, in the battle of Leningrad, but it moves us to the center of the historical stage, uncontested. We're a power now. And the shape of what has been bequeathed to us in terms of our present crisis becomes clear to us in the form first and foremost of an unprecedented economic boom from 1945 to 1973. The unprecedented economic boom in the shaping of the American pyramidal social structure into a diamond, a mass middle-class with a mass culture with a formula of mass production and mass consumption. But having also to respond to that other crucial world historical process, the decolonization of the Third World: 1947 in India, China in '49, Ghana in '57, Cuba in '59, Guinea in '60. It's a different world. Martin Luther King, Jr. looks to India to break the back of apartheid like a rule of law in the southern part of this first new nation, with its institutionalized discourse of whiteness and blackness. Whiteness positively charged, blackness negatively valued.

This would fundamentally shape what it means to be an American. Sicilian peasants would come and discover they're white. That was in the process of becoming an American. It's a construct, a social construct, but deeply sedimented and saturated in the everyday life of the first new nation. Malcolm X would look to Africa, to Ghana. There was a sense of possibilities. It's hard to capture that sense of possibilities now, although here at Berkeley it should be easier than most places. It's hard to capture that moment now of this unprecedented economic boom, world hegemony, the subordination of Latin American markets, as a support of usually anti-democratic regimes to ensure access to those markets. The Marshall Plan: rebuilding Europe against the Red Menace, the Red Threat, and to provide new markets for American products. These are the 28 years which serve as a backdrop against which we compare our present moment.

What is very important to keep in mind, when we think about prospects for democracy, is that the time between 1945 and 1973 is the period in which the nation state was in fact deployed to create a mass middle class. Unemployment compensation, worker's comp., social security, Federal Housing Administration, the G.I. Bill—what would America have been without these? That's part of the welfare state. That's one reason Eisenhower didn't contest it the same way Tories in Canada don't contest the National Health Care service system, because it's part of the consensus. You can see how far the discourse has shifted in the last fifteen years. But it's a moment, then, in which, for the first time, some black folks had to make their bid into the middle classes, the racial caste system still operating rather strongly even after the Supreme Court had put forth its May 19, 1954, *Brown v. Board of Education*. Later, women, gays and lesbians and Latinos would bring their critique to bear, catalyzed by a sense of collective insurgency that Professor Lasch in his paper was describing so well in the Civil Rights movement, grounded in black civil society, and especially in the black churches.

But 1945 to '73 is a kind of golden age now both for capital as well as for the majority of Americans who then had a conception of their government as a government that, one, could do something and two, could help them. But in 1973 there is a decline in the level of productivity, fragility of the bank structure as the debt of the Third World nations escalated, OPEC, the rise of a Third World in control of one of the major resources that would sustain an industrial order. And we all know that if Kuwait specialized in artichokes rather than oil, Mr. Bush would not have moved so quickly. 1973 is a very different moment, economic contraction. And what's distinctive about 1973 in terms of our present moment is three features: the need for restructuring of the economy, capitalist restructuring, deindustrialization. Steelworkers, boom! Rubberworkers, boom! Steelworkers are cut in half in nine years, now nearly disappeared. Rubberworkers, autoworkers, the manufacturing heartland is devastated by the need to restructure owing to a very different moment. Competition with the Germans, at that time, the West Germans, the Japanese, the merging Four Tigers—Taiwan, Hong Kong, Singapore, South Korea—not only the industrialization but also deregulation that was emerging, not solely under Reagan but already with major pushers.

Politically, that's very important to keep in mind. I think Thomas Edsall and Mary Edsall are absolutely right in the story they tell, even though I disagree with the conclusion they draw from it (we can talk about that later). There is a realignment of the American voting public, in which issues of race linked to the welfare state, the racial coding of the nation state, so that when the state does something for someone, it becomes excessively associated with that state doing it for black folk and women.

It wasn't solely about race but primarily. It's about busing, racially coded conceptions of Title VII, later to become debates about affirmative action, and especially—this is a real challenge for Professor Lasch—about place, residential segregation, red-lining by banks, which is of course the very basis for the inability of desegregated education to ever become a reality in the urban centers, you see. It has something to do, sure, with behavior and pathologies and so on, but residential segregation—that's why King lost in Chicago in 1965. He couldn't break the back of it; he cried, it brought tears to his eyes. And no one has broken the back of it yet. That's what the malls are, white folk getting away, all those black folk who have middle-class status getting away.

Understandably so, because when we look indeed at the fundamental feature of what we've experienced in the last eighteen years, it is the 19.1 percent decline in real wages of the working Americans, inflation-adjusted wages. That's downward mobility, that's social slippage. When it becomes linked to the spiritual impoverishment, the spiritual sterility of cultural consumption, you've got something lethal on your hands. You've got the makings of right-wing politics. It's true. And we thank God it hasn't become excessively fascist, owing to some of the residues of the best of the liberal tradition, and some of us Democratic Socialists are still out there fighting. Because under other circumstances it could easily have become excessively fascist, as we're seeing now, with Le Pen in France and the Lombard League in Italy and the skinheads in Germany. We have had for eighteen years what Wallace Peterson has called "the silent depression." At the same time it is then reinforced by the most massive redistribution of wealth from working people to the well-to-do; regressive taxation after '81. This is a devastated population we're talking about, across races. It's not just the cutbacks in the social programs or the slow-downs in the programs, or the take-backs at the negotiation tables between capital and labor, or the build-ups in the military budget, but larger structural tendencies, that have now squeezed the majority of American people while the top 2 percent have had a party, given regressive taxation. And where are we now? Relative national decline.

Those who had the party didn't save as was claimed by the supply-side economists. Unprecedented private and public debt, the government can't move.

We have a whole new subculture among capitalists. I'm sure many of you read this in Michael Levine's book, *The Money Culture*; short term profiteering, speculation, merger. He writes about a chap who made $550 million in one year, that wasn't enough, he'd take the risk of going to jail to make $555. Something is going on psychologically there. It's a different culture at work. You can talk to those "poor people" within the subculture of that highbrow, upper echelons of capital to discover this. In fact, a lot of them are getting born-again because they figure, maybe I'd better get some spiritual resources to deal with all the corruption and greed and so forth and so on. But most importantly, with a stubborn incapacity to generate resources, the public square is one of squalor, opulence reigns supreme. No taxes, there's only three ways you can raise money: You divert money you already have from the military budget, or somewhere else. You borrow it, that's in fact what has been going on—military Keynesianism under Reagan, John Maynard is not dead. Up until 1991 with the S&Ls. You can't borrow any more now. Three hundred billion dollars every year for the next four years. You can't borrow any more. S&L. Or you tax. President Bush says no taxes. My governor said taxes and you saw what happened, Mr. Florio you see. It was badly done P.R.-wise, but he had the right idea. Hemorrhage, then, in the government.

And then at the level of lived experience, the cultural decay, the erosion of civil society that Professor Lasch discussed so well. The shattering of families, neighborhoods, churches, mosques, synagogues, civic associations, leading toward the slow breakdown of the nurturing systems for children. This is very important for children, although Professor Lasch and I may disagree on how we end up generating new ways for nurturing children. And we're not just talking about one out of five in poverty, or one out of two black and two out of five brown children in poverty, we're talking about the state of their souls, the inability to transmit meaning, value, purpose, dignity, decency, elegance, excellence, to children. They become deracinated, rootless, delimited, culturally naked. By culturally naked what I mean is, unable to navigate through the inescapable traumas and unavoidable terrors of human life, of death, of disease, of disappointment, of dread, of despair. Every human being has to be equipped or, as Durkheim said, culture doesn't work. You kill yourself or somebody else. In one vulgar sense culture is an attempt to convince you not to kill yourself or someone else. Look at our homicide rate. Cultural breakdown, escalating self-destructive nihilism among the poor and very poor. We have experienced a meaninglessness and hopelessness and most important, lovelessness. At the bodily level. What is it like to live years and never be touched with compassion? What a life. Increasing self-paralyzing pessimism among the stable working and lower middle classes. A pessimism regarding their sense of the future, but America is the land of the future. We don't believe the future will be better. Discontinuous with so much; the American past, not the black American past, not much of the southern American past, but much of the American past, discontinuous, the future won't be better? My God! Self-indulgent hedonism, self-serving cynicism of the well-to-do, which does in fact include a number of our fellow academicians. They're professional managers like anybody else, no matter what their rhetoric at times. The luxury, the privilege, serves as a basis upon which they choose the work they do. This is not a put-down of them, it's a description. Because they make choices. I do believe in accountability and personal responsibility, people make choices but not under circumstances of their own choosing. They do make choices though.

This leads us where then? Raising the issue. How do we talk about prospects for democracy? This is where Lippmann comes in and this is a set of queries that I want to raise for my friends who spent dear moments of their short lives writing that lovely book. I am not convinced that Walter Lippmann provides the kind of resources you want for your own democratic project. I read their book in May, it took me back to the library to read Mr. Lippmann. Given my own Democratic Left tradition, I had read *A Preface to Politics* and *Drifting Mastery*. That's 1913 and 1914, early Lippmann, under the influence of James, in some way influenced by Debs, but he thinks Debs is too much of an evangelical idealist in his socialist activity. He is not only full of hope but full of the democratic faith that Whitman had, making this Pascalian leap of faith in the mental and moral capacities of ordinary people, so that they ought to participate in the institutions that guide and regulate their lives, especially the decision-making processes in those institutions. And it is a leap of faith, the evidence is always under-determined in relation to ordinary folk like ourselves, I'm including all of us. All of us feeble creatures, with faults and foibles and having to face death, that's ordinary enough for me. It is a Pascalian leap of faith.

But by 1922 Lippmann gives this faith up. The legacy of August of 1914 is too much. Like Eliot in *The Waste Land*, like Joyce in *Ulysses*, he gives up on history rooted in ordinary people's agency. He begins to talk about myths and symbols, the ways in which ordinary people are manipulated and how gullible they are, and the fundamental role of prejudice, indifference and apathy. In that text, *Public Opinion*, published in 1922, you get this fundamental break in Lippmann. One chapter is on stereotypes—how human beings always think in terms of stereotypes and public opinion is nothing but a moralizing, codified version of facts based on stereotypes that none of us can step outside of. This is his claim in that text. And his response to that problem is that we must give up on the very notion of self-government. It's a radical text. Keep in mind, old Abe Lincoln used to say "Self-government is better than good government." I think he's right. I mean, Russia after Nicholas II, he had Alexander II, looked like he had a decent chap, right? After all those ugly anti-semitic decrees that Nicholas had, Alexander seemed a benevolent despot. And then comes Alexander III after the assassination, right back into the ugliness. No self-government or accountability over it. That's what Lincoln had in mind, you see. Lippmann says no. And it's very revealing that Lippmann begins that text with a reference to Book 7, Plato's *Republic,* that majestic allegory of the cave where human beings confuse things with shadows. There's a chain within that cave with the fire burning. And lo and behold, at the very end of that text, "it's true," he says, "the only way we can get out of this is putting forward some notion of organized intelligence of a society run by the experts." In *The Phantom Public* of 1925, three years later, he builds upon the same claim, and this is what upsets John Dewey, the great follower of Whitman.

Dewey writes *The Public and Its Problems* in 1927. And yes, he trots out the old, trite cliché, "the cure for the ills of democracy is more democracy," but what he has in mind is trying to generate a politics of constituting a public sphere that overlaps with the proliferation of other publics that allow for what is the basic theme in that book, which is one of public communication. The problem is not that there's no public, the problem is that there's so many different publics. Dewey says they're market-driven publics in the United States but there's no overlap of these publics so that communication can take place. Without communication it reinforces balkanization and fragmentation and ghettoization and marginalization of the various publics. It sounds similar to our own day. We're certainly in a highly balkanized and fragmented moment. But what's fascinating about Lippmann is that he poses a question that no democrat, to my mind, has adequately answered. Not Dewey, not my good friends here, Michael Harrington, or a whole host of democrats. The challenge is: Is it the case that in a market culture it's possible to sustain democratic sensibilities? Is it not the case, Lippmann says, that education does become entertainment, that the trivial and the eccentric and the idiosyncratic does in fact become that which sells because it titillates and it stimulates. That's one of the reasons why you see so much of the sensationalizing of racial conflict. Racial conflict has been around for a long time. But I know in New York City we've got some newspapers who are in deep trouble, very deep trouble. Of course there's some ugly xenophobia, ugly black anti-semitism, ugly white racism, ugly homophobia; they just killed this brother, this gay Hispanic brother, Julio Rivera. Skinheads. For the fun of it. That's there. But that's always been there. But the sensationalizing, for market purposes, to sustain it, will sell newspapers. Leonard Jeffrey is on the cover of the *New York Post* every other week. Every time he's on there they sell almost twice as many copies. We're not talking about argument, we're not talking about quality of exchange, critical exchange and so forth, you see. Lippmann's point is: how do you convince persons in a market culture that democratic sensibilities like critical engagement, like talking about ambiguous legacies of civilization rather than monolithic and homogeneous characterizations of civilizations, are relevant? Hybrid cultures, rather than pure and pristine cultures. How do you get beyond the Manichean perspective and either/or options in such a culture? Lippmann says "I cannot imagine it, I'm sorry, I'm no longer a serious democrat, it doesn't make sense." That's a serious challenge. I don't know of a democrat who's responded to it. Some of us bank our lives on trying to provide evidence to respond to. But I don't know anybody who's responded. Dewey didn't at all in that text. He just held up the Great Community at the end, but it has no base. In one sense that's the question I would ask Professor Lasch. I'll ask him tomorrow. I'll push him tomorrow. I'll ask him now. One wants to know what sits beneath the populism. Is there any politics there or is it resignation? Are there any sources for hope on the ground? Not just the arguments which often times for me are very persuasive. Professor Lasch has been persuasive ever since he wrote *The Agony of the American Left* on a variety of different issues, and utterly unpersuasive on others, but we'll talk about that tomorrow.

My point is, I'm using him as an example in terms of Dewey's project. There's a certain impotence that Dewey felt as a radical democrat. And my challenge to the authors of *The Good Society* who would want to appropriate Lippmann is: Is it the challenge in Lippmann that you want? That's fine with me. But if it's an appropriation of what's in Lippmann for your democratic project I'm unconvinced. The title of the book, *The Good Society*, comes out of Lippmann's 1937 book and I actually did get a chance to get a look at that book and it is a book that has Lippmann very much leaning toward the right of his day. He had just given the Godkin lecture of 1935 called "The Method of Freedom," that Arthur Schlesinger, Jr. praised because it defended the New Deal. But there's a fundamental reversal in Lippmann's career. In *The Good Society* he trashes the New Deal. He says it's on a continuum with the other collectivisms in the world like fascism. Earlier he had made a distinction between military collectivism, fascism and free collectivism when he supported Roosevelt. But he changes his mind. He even voted for Governor Landon in '36, against Roosevelt. And what does he go back to with a deep nostalgia? Common Law, Coke, Belden, Blackstone. This is not the most radical crowd that I know of. To defend what? Civility. What he calls the great traditions of civility. He invokes Ernest Barker, even, in that text where that phrase comes from. But he also defends liberty and this is why Adam Smith is the hero. But civility and liberty are conservative perspectives because he never raises the fundamental issue that the New Deal was all about. Namely, how are we going to deal with these human beings who are bearing this social cost of the crisis? The one-third who are ill-fed and ill-sheltered and ill-housed? Lippmann never raises that question. He talks about division of labor, "we're all interdependent" and so forth and so on. But he never raises a deeper, structural question of how would you then deal with those who are bearing the social cost?

And that's what's striking about *The Good Society* in 1991, because these authors are fundamentally concerned with that question. That's what puts them in the democratic tradition, it's what puts them with Dewey over and against Lippmann. But to appropriate his title seems to me to require a stronger argument as to what you're really teasing out of Walter Lippmann. Is it the internationalism that you like? If that's so, Lippmann's internationalism was quite narrow. There is no talk about the role of colonies, which is fundamental. Take a book like Du Bois's *Color and Democracy: Colonies and Peace*, published in 1945, which is a direct challenge to Lippmann's I.R. School, the International Relations School. No engagement with him. You believe in conversation? Respond to the critique! You believe in critical exchange? Respond to the critique! The silences and the blindnesses in the text, that's what I'm talking about. Now these same silences and blindnesses are alluded to in *The Good Society*, but as I suggested I wanted to see more. Bob Bellah has given me his remarks and I will read them tonight because there are in fact attempts to be even more specific. The gestures are there in the text, much more so than in *Habits of the Heart*. I must say I like *The Good Society* so much more than *Habits of the Heart*, but that's my own humble opinion. The gestures are there but they are not concretely fleshed out. And by concretely fleshed out I don't mean a blueprint, I mean the analysis has to be focused on where in fact those social costs are being borne and what the responses are. We're not talking about human beings as victims here, we're talking about victimization being in place and about responses to that victimization.

Let me end by saying something about where I think one could go in talking about prospects for democracy. First and foremost I think we have to speak to what I call the spiritual impoverishment. We have to speak to the social breakdown that generates a distancing of human beings from hope and courage and discipline and risk-taking. That's a deep cultural renaissance and it's vertical as well as horizontal. I talked about it in terms of the politics of conversion in my *Dissent* essay on nihilism in black America a few months ago. The politics of conversion is based on a love ethic. The only way people in fact overcome nihilism (because nihilism is a disease of the soul just like alcoholism and drug addiction), the only way you overcome it is by means of love and care. There's no other way. Love in one's relationships, love in a cause, a political cause, a political movement, or love in religious community or a community that takes seriously non-market values like love, care, justice. Remember those? Love, care, solidarity, and so forth. And in fact, just a quick footnote about Sweden. I think the important point about Sweden's welfare state is that it uses solidaristic policy, to hold the market at arm's length so that basic social goods aren't simply commodities. That's something different than a welfare state that's parasitical on corporate profit and a weak state. There's a different motivation. I think that's much of the best of the democratic social movement, though I have my criticisms of it.

But let me end by saying something about the prospects. First at this cultural level. It's a cultural renaissance that's needed for persons to believe that non-market values can and will make a difference. And you only do that by generating social momentum. And you generate social momentum by creating networks, later on mobilizing, possibly organizing and, if you're lucky, creating a social movement. This is the best the Left has ever done in the conservative American society where the sacred cow is economic growth by means of corporate priorities and in a society that is chronically, like most societies we know, xenophobic; a deeply racist, patriarchal, homophobic, anti-semitic and so forth. The only terrain for the Left has been generating that social motion and possibly creating a social movement, to be crushed for the most part, given the powers that be. But making a difference in the meantime. What I would argue, for the prospects of democracy, is on the one hand, creating conditions for the possibility of social momentum and social motion. The problem, of course, is it gets out of hand. From 1964 to 1968, 329 rebellions in 257 cities. That made a difference. But it was out of hand. Much of it pre-political, just sheer, existential rebellion, producing chaos. Capital can't function in such chaotic situations. But it made a difference. Acts of desperation with no political direction, no leadership of integrity that could direct them. But that is social motion, believe me. Undirected, unbuffeted, but that's social motion. The other side is working with the elites in place, and working with the elites in place means then trying to ensure both public investment and expanding universal social programs. Is this old-style welfare statism? I would say not at all. Some economists argue that over 40 percent of the decline of productivity in America is because its infrastructures are deteriorating. We're talking about moving bodies, like highways, shipping goods on waterways, trains, trucks, and of course schools, not the kids in them we are talking about, just the buildings themselves. Public investment is about sustaining the level of investment in infrastructure. That contestation takes place within the state. In the last fifteen years the United States has averaged 1.1 percent of investment in infrastructure; Germany averages 3.1 percent. Think about that. It's not just that the workers are more educated; in fact they are, they're better educated. But that's not solely it. It has something to do with infrastructure, but in addition, public works programs.

Other layers generate dependency. I think some of the neo-conservatives are right about that. But first on the ground, there needs to be some response to the massive redistribution of resources from those below to those above, given the massive implications that that has had for so many of our fellow citizens. Social programs. Medicare made a difference for old people. That's not dependency, that's providing a social provision for someone in need. An expansion of such programs, programs that are not in any way targeted to certain groups such that right-wing politicians can take advantage of them. That's one of the real sources of hope in Wofford's victory in Pennsylvania. There's some down sides to it that we can talk about as well. That's the kind of focused issue, it seems to me, that's necessary to talk concretely about prospects of democracy. National health care is another. I think now with Magic Johnson contracting the HIV virus that maybe some of the elites will wake up and discover that thousands of their fellow citizens could possibly be on the road to recovery if they would provide more resources, if they were serious about that as they were about oil profits in the Middle East. That's a possible source of social motion. The problem is going to be, what is the quality of leadership? The problem is going to be, what kind of vision and analysis would allow for these various groups on the ground that are working so that they can overlap enough to generate a social motion and possible social movement? That's the hope, it's always dangling, but as long as there's some movement it seems to me, we can sustain that.

Let me end with a quote from one of the coninical pillars, this is again brother Walt, in 1871. He says:

> Judging from the main portions of the history of the world so far, justice is always in jeopardy, peace walks amid hourly pitfalls and of slavery, misery, meanness, the craft of tyrants and the credulity of the populace, in some of their protean forms, no voice can at any times say 'They are not pervasive.' The cloud breaks a little and the sun shines out but soon and certain the lowering darkness falls again as if to last forever. Yet is there an immortal courage and prophesy in every sane soul that cannot, must not, under any circumstances capitulate. Viva the attack! The perennial assault. Viva the unpopular cause, the spirit that audaciously aims, the never abandoned effort pursued the same amid opposing proofs and precedents.

That's the tradition, the radical tradition of hope. Not

naïve, not optimistic, but of hope. A prisoner and purveyor of hope was Whitman. That's what's necessary. I thank the Good Society Project for providing me the occasion for this kind of dialogue and I thank all those fellow strugglers of hope, my good friend Michael Lerner from *Tikkun* magazine, the whole host of black preachers struggling in New York, bringing critique to bear although it never surfaces in the press on a moral level. Brother Larry Rasmussen knows what I'm talking about. James Forbes can condemn the murder of Rosenbaum and it never surfaces. And then they say the black community is silent and try to paint the black community with a brush of immorality. That kind of struggle against the hopelessness that seems to be so pervasive is that upon which we build. As T.S. Eliot says, "for us there is only the trying—the rest is not our business."

About Common Courage Press

Books for an Informed Democracy

In this volume, Cornel West argues that

...we must move beyond the debate over eurocentrism and multiculturalism, calling into question all notions of pure traditions or pristine heritages, or any civilization or culture having a monopoly on virtue or insight. We must accent boldly, and defiantly, the gap between principles and practice, between promise and performance, between rhetoric and reality. And in these desperate times we must grapple with human hope: to engage in an audacious attempt to galvanize and energize, to inspire and to invigorate world weary people.

In an effort to work toward this perspective, Common Courage Press was founded in 1991 and publishes books for social justice on race, gender, feminism, economics, ecology, indigenous issues, labor, and U.S. domestic and foreign policy. The Press seeks to provide analysis of problems from a range of perspectives and to aid activists and others in developing strategies for action.

You can reach us at:

Common Courage Press
P.O. Box 702
Monroe, ME 04951
207-525-0900 fax: 207-525-3068

Send for a free catalog!